Battle for the
FIØRDS

NATO's Forward Maritime Strategy in Action

ERIC GROVE
with Graham Thompson

LONDON
IAN ALLAN LTD

First published 1991

ISBN 0 7110 1922 3

© Eric Grove 1991

Published by Ian Allan Ltd,
Shepperton, Surrey; and printed
by Ian Allan Printing Ltd at their
works at Coombelands in
Runnymede, England

Below:
CV-66 *America* cruising through typical fiord scenery.

Contents

Preface

Although Teamwork '88 happened two years ago it remains the best example to date of the forward maritime strategy in action. Because of the Gulf Crisis, Teamwork '90 was much reduced, a great disappointment to the NATO planners who had originally intended something even larger than the 1988 exercise. Despite the recent and welcome transformation in East-West relations, the need for such exercises as the Teamwork series remains. They are now perhaps even more important, for the dissolution of the Warsaw Pact means that Supreme Allied Commander Atlantic rather than SACEUR is the main Western front line commander. He confronts a Russian maritime capability that is reducing in quantity but improving greatly in quality. Because of American reluctance to constrain the power of their navy we still have to address the problems of defusing the Cold War confrontation at sea, especially in northern waters. Indeed it may never disappear entirely. Because of sheer geography Norway will continue to feel threatened by the concentration of Russian strength in the Kola Peninsula. She will need the reassurance of Western maritime power, regularly exercised to demonstrate its effectiveness. Similarly, as long as Europe feels the need to maintain its strategic links with the USA a vital means of safeguarding the Atlantic link will be to place NATO's battlefleet in Norwegian waters. Indeed, reductions in American naval strength will make this forward strategy more rather than less important as escort forces are drawn down and peacetime power projection predominates as the role of the forces that remain. The battle for the fiords will remain a key factor in the control of the sea communications that are the foundation of Western security.

Acknowledgements

Never has an author relied more on outside help than in the writing of this book. Adm Sir Julian Oswald when British CINCFLEET and NATO CINCHAN and CINCEASTLANT provided essential support and encouragement throughout the project. Without him and his staff the book would have been neither begun nor completed. Adm Hugo White, then Flag Officer Third Flotilla and NATO COMASWSTRIK-FOR, and his amazingly efficient staff gave me facilities to observe and understand the exercise that could not have been bettered. The officers and men of HMS *Illustrious*, many of them former colleagues and students, could not have been more gracious hosts at a busy time for them all. Adm Redd of the Standing Naval Force Atlantic, Cdr Stan Weeks and the officers and men of the USS *Hayler* were also extraordinarily generous with their hospitality and tolerance as were Capt Eric Ernst and his crew in the cruiser *South Carolina*. No one could have treated a stranger, quite literally dropped in on them, with more genuine warmth than the men of 'Socar' whose Chiefs paid me the signal honour of making me an honorary chief petty officer in the US Navy. Finally I must thank Cdr Kristensen, the convoy commodore, and Capt John Nichols and the crew of the *Criscilla* who were perfect hosts in the coastal convoy. The public relations staff of the relevant NATO commands provided unstinting support throughout and special mention must be made of Lt-Cdr Phil Whalley RN and Cdr Wolf Moebus FGN who were my main liaison officers at Northwood and Norfolk respectively. A full list of those who helped would fill a book; to all many thanks, but especially to Linda Cullen for assistance with pictures and my parents for helping produce the typescript. Graham Thompson wrote Chapter 6 and contributed material to Chapter 8. He also would like to thank NATO's public relations staff for arranging his visit to Norway to cover the exercise.

Eric Grove
Morden, 1991

Foreword

By Flag Officer Scotland and Northern Ireland

At first sight a book on NATO Exercise 'Teamwork 88' as an example of the Alliance's Forward Maritime Strategy may appear to be a subject chosen by a specialist for specialists, with some danger of being overtaken by subsequent momentous events within the Soviet empire. Such a first impression, however, would be misleading. Eric Grove has a deep understanding of maritime strategic issues, and their historic application. He analyses the growth of the forward defence strategy in the 1980s and projects its application into the decade ahead where he believes its principles will continue to apply even more crucially in a less certain world. His thesis will appeal to any layman interested in the defence strategic scene, but his analysis goes beyond strategy.

He embarked in the NATO Striking Fleet throughout the exercise, moving, sometimes not without hazard, from ship to ship. Drawing on his already comprehensive understanding of maritime warfare at tactical level, he was able to compile a broad and accurate picture of the progress of the exercise; no small achievement in the real and metaphorical fog which so often surrounded the action. His grasp of combat essentials from the crucial nature of electronic warfare to the subtleties of modern anti-submarine tactics enables him to comment on the unfolding battle in a way which will both stimulate the non-professional reader and reveal new dimensions to experts. I was fortunate in having him on board HMS *Illustrious*, the ASW Striking Force Flagship, for a protracted spell during the Striking Fleet's transit of the Iceland-Faeroes-UK gaps. His enthusiasm was infectious. Given half a chance I know he would have enjoyed taking over and would no doubt have put his theories into efficient practice. As it was, the exercise enthralled him and he filled notebook after notebook with observations. This book is therefore based on an authentic inside story.

What comes over so well in these pages is the linkage between strategy and its practical application at sea; the huge environmental arena measured horizontally in hundreds of miles and vertically from space to the ocean floor; and the NATO Striking Fleet's size and power, demonstrating the dominant strength of the United States Navy as well as the large numbers of submarines, ships and aircraft from many NATO nations working together in a highly co-ordinated enterprise, capable of great flexibility in pursuit of its aims. This short book gives an unusually clear insight into the complexities, strengths and weaknesses of modern naval warfare at the highest level. For those concerned with the balance between the minimum price for defence and our requirement for future security, it is a good starting point from which to consider the need for continued application of maritime power as a force to promote peace and stability in a changing — and potentially still dangerous — world.

H. M. White
Vice-Admiral
Commander Anti-Submarine
Warfare Striking Force, 1987-88

1 NATO's Forward Maritime Strategy

During the 1980s NATO had been more explicit than ever before about how it planned to fight at sea should the Alliance fail in its primary purpose of deterrence. This led to much debate about a 'new' Maritime Strategy emphasising forward operations in the Norwegian Sea. Critics of the Forward Strategy have argued that it is dangerous on a number of grounds: that it exposes Western forces to unnecessary risks; that it is unduly provocative of the Soviet Union; that it will lead to premature escalation to nuclear war; and that it forgets the lessons of history that the major sea control effort against a submarine and air threat should be around the assets at risk, ie the vital shipping bringing reinforcements and supplies across the Atlantic. Much of this critique rests on some misleading assumptions about the Forward Maritime Strategy. This book will attempt to describe the reality of forward operations as exercised in September 1988

Below:
NATO's Striking Fleet at birth. It was first gathered together for Exercise 'Main Brace' in September 1952 forming up in the Clyde to move to Norway's defence. It contained four US strike carriers, among them the USS *Midway* seen on the left of the picture and her sister ship the *Franklin D. Roosevelt*. Ahead of the *Midway* is one of the two battleships, USS *Wisconsin* (the other was HMS *Vanguard*). Britain contributed two fleet carriers and a light carrier, HMS *Theseus*, seen in the right foreground. The latter ship formed part of an ASW carrier support group with the Canadian carrier *Magnificent* and an American ASW carrier. 'Main Brace' was a major show of maritime power on NATO's northern flank and in all, over 100 major warships were involved in it. The exercise demonstrated the essential nature of NATO's Maritime Strategy right from the start, the use of maritime power projection both to defend the northern allies and to attack the Soviet Northern Fleet 'at source'. *USNI*

NATO's Maritime Strategy as originally conceived

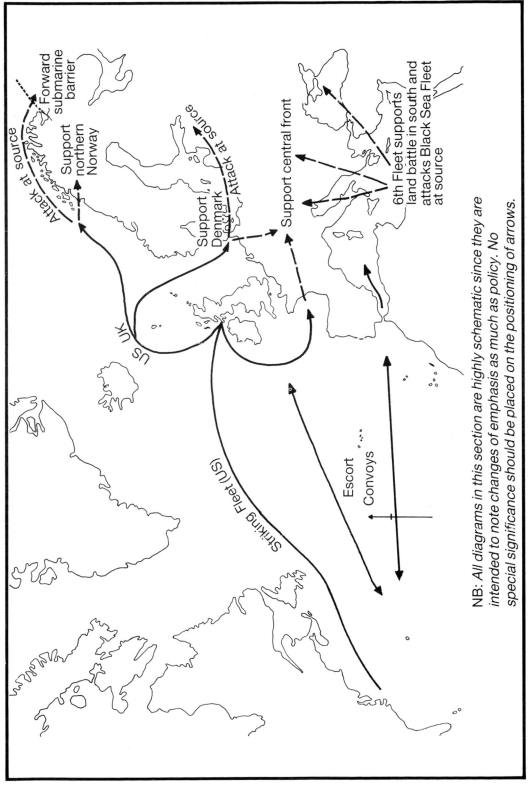

Forward submarine barrier

Attack at source

Support northern Norway

Attack at source

Support Denmark

Support central front

6th Fleet supports land battle in south and attacks Black Sea Fleet at source

US UK

Striking Fleet (US)

Escort Convoys

NB: All diagrams in this section are highly schematic since they are intended to note changes of emphasis as much as policy. No special significance should be placed on the positioning of arrows.

Above:
'Main Brace' saw an experiment with an Anglo-American 'Hunter-Killer Force' for anti-submarine (ASW) composed of an American ASW carrier and seven specialist fast ASW ships. These included Britain's pair of experimental Type 15 fast frigates converted from fleet destroyers, HMS *Relentless* seen here and HMS *Rocket* (right). The five American 'Gearing' class ships were converted to 'DDE' ASW configuration such as the USS *Rich* (left). The conflict between using ASW forces for escort purposes or for supposedly more 'offensive' tasks has been a constant theme in the debate over NATO's maritime strategy. The picture was taken from the escort carrier USS *Salerno Bay*. The ship in the right background appears to be the light fleet carrier USS *Wright*, part of the main carrier striking force. *USNI*

in Exercise 'Teamwork'. This showed NATO's strategy as it might be applied in action although, of course, operations in an actual crisis would depend heavily on the scenario. All that can be done in peacetime is to exercise options. Indeed, the 'Norwegian Sea Campaign' is but one of five campaigns in NATO's Concept of Maritime Operations, usually known as CONMAROPS. The other four are the 'Atlantic', the 'Shallow Seas', the 'Mediterranean Lifelines' and 'Eastern Mediterranean', and all are interdependent with each other and with operations ashore. Nevertheless, given the need to allocate priorities to scarce resources, it is clear that the Alliance currently puts greatest stress on forward operations in the Norwegian Sea as its potential means to keep neutralised the most dangerous concentration of Soviet maritime power, the Northern Fleet. If the latter can be tied down in defensive operations and/or destroyed in combat, it would not be available to intervene in the other campaigns; thus these can be fought on as favourable terms as possible.

Essentially there is nothing at all new in NATO's naval forces thinking in terms of forward operations. As soon as it was formed the Alliance committed itself to defending its members wherever threatened. Norway was a founder member of NATO and was determined to assure itself of the protection of its allies. This required Anglo-American maritime power to be available for forward defence of this area including possible reinforcement ashore. Moreover the leading navy in NATO, that of the United States, with its World War 2 experience in the Pacific region, was firmly committed to the concept of using a striking fleet of aircraft carriers to destroy the enemy 'at source' in his bases. Already the quantity and quality of the postwar Soviet submarine force was casting shadows over NATO's ability to repeat the success of the convoy and escort strategy of 1939-45. It was recognised that during World War 2 purely conventional bombing attacks had been useless in reducing the U-boat threat but, in the early 1950s, US carrier aircraft were beginning to be equipped with nuclear weapons that would be much more effective, even against hardened submarine pens. In addition the striking fleet would contain an amphibious component to put ashore to reinforce the outnumbered local defenders. NATO's first Supreme Allied Commander Atlantic (SACLANT), appointed in 1952, Adm Lynde McCormick USN, lost no time in asserting that he had no intention of being tied down to a purely defensive operational concept.

To demonstrate a capacity both to defend Norway and to threaten the Soviet Navy in its bases, NATO's very first major Atlantic exercise in 1952, 'Main Brace', consisted of carrier operations off Vestfiord. At the Exercise press conference it was emphasised that NATO needed to be able to operate off northern Norway and that her maritime exercises could not be restricted to small areas. No less than four American and two British fleet carriers were deployed for 'Main Brace', together with three light carriers — one British, one American and one Canadian. Amphibious landings were carried out — albeit in Denmark rather than Norway. The following year the Striking

Fleet operated further south but its central, offensive role in any future Atlantic battle was re-emphasised. In 1954 Lord Ismay, NATO's first Secretary General, stated that the Striking Fleet would 'undertake offensive and support operations rather than direct defence of Atlantic trade routes'. He also emphasised its support role to other NATO commanders, including Supreme Allied Commander Europe (SACEUR).

Below:
In the early days of NATO the British could only effectively provide fighter and ASW cover to the Striking Fleet given the limited striking potential of their carrier air groups. During 'Main Brace' the Second Carrier Group (here seen in line ahead) was formed of HMS *Eagle* carrying two squadrons of Attacker jet fighters, two Firefly ASW squadrons and a Firebrand strike squadron; HMS *Illustrious* with a Firefly ASW squadron, a Dutch Firefly ASW squadron and a Dutch Sea Fury fighter squadron; and the USS *Wright*, a fast light fleet carrier carrying Corsair fighters and Skyraider attack aircraft. *Illustrious* was normally used as the Trials and Training Carrier but was mobilised annually for exercises. The Striking Fleet role and the influence Carrier Group Two gave over the operations of the whole Fleet, was the key factor in maintaining a British carrier fleet at this time. It still carries considerable force today when British naval policy and procurement are being considered. *Imperial War Museum*

At this time the planned wartime composition of the Striking Fleet was as follows: (D+30 days)

- Fleet Carriers 6 (2 British, 4 American)
- Battleships 2 (1 British, 1 American)
- Cruisers 8 (4 British, 4 American)
- Destroyers 36 (15 British, 21 American)
- Submarines would also be allocated in direct support.

Then, as now, the British ships, as in-theatre assets, were expected to be deployed earlier than the American. Despite this important role, however, because of Royal Navy competition with the Royal Air Force (RAF) over who should attack targets ashore, Britain's contribution to the Striking Fleet became a matter of some dispute in Whitehall. In a hard-fought battle that went on throughout 1953 and 1954 the Admiralty was able to assert the continued need for a British Striking Fleet contribution as the Royal Navy's major wartime commitment. This remained the case even after the 1957 Defence Review. Although Mr Duncan Sandys, the Defence Minister, disapproved of the Striking Fleet concept (as Minister of Supply he had masterminded the previous attack on the carriers) the Royal Navy was able to argue to the Government that as long as NATO still believed in the Striking Fleet, Britain could not renage on her commitment to provide a significant part of it. In these early days the British role in the Striking Fleet was largely fighter and anti-submarine protection, but the acquisition of nuclear weapons by the Royal Navy's Scimitar carrier-based fighters after the 'Red Beard' bomb went into production in 1959 meant that the British

Below:
By the late 1950s the emphasis in Striking Fleet operations had become distinctly nuclear, as was emphasised by the name of the 1957 major NATO maritime exercise in Arctic waters, 'Strike Back'. Here operating with two of her smaller sisters is the first American super carrier USS *Forrestal*, her decks crammed with four of her aircraft types, the FJ-3 Fury fighter, the F-3H Demon fighter, the AD Skyraider attack aircraft and the A-3D Skywarrior heavy attack aircraft; she also carried F-8U Crusaders. With the development of lightweight nuclear weapons a wide range of carrier types had become nuclear capable, including fighters, and even the piston-engined Skyraiders. The Skywarriors posed a major threat to targets deep inside the Soviet Union. The emphasis on 'spasm' nuclear operations emphasised still more the striking fleet and power projection aspects of NATO maritime strategy rather than the traditional defence of shipping role in more protracted naval warfare. *Forrestal* would return to northern waters 31 years later to take part in Exercise 'Teamwork' with a rather different scenario. On both occasions she came from duty with the Sixth Fleet in the Mediterranean, a good example of the flexibility of carrier operations. *USNI*

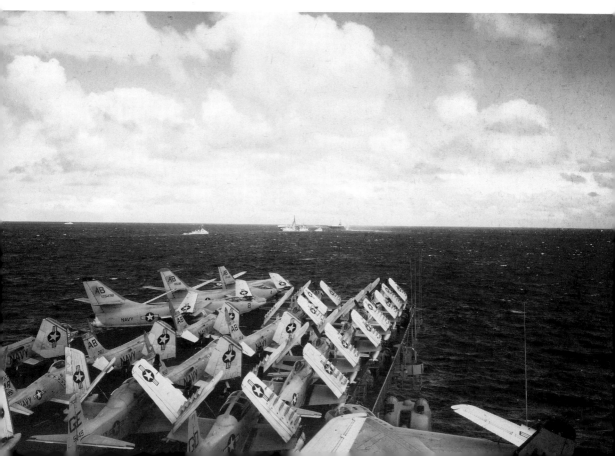

The Nuclear Era

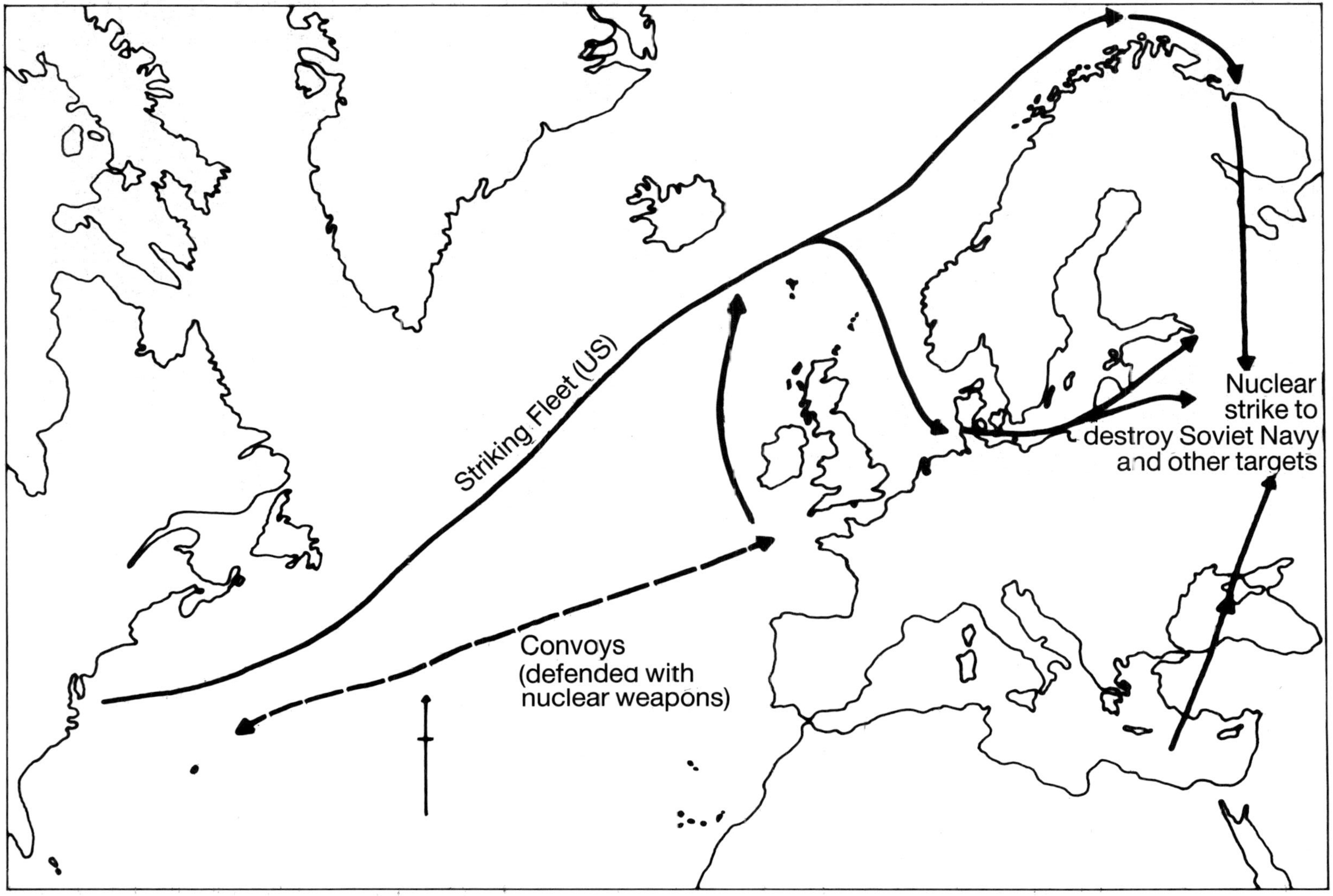

Nuclear strike to destroy Soviet Navy and other targets

Striking Fleet (US)

Convoys (defended with nuclear weapons)

carrier contribution became in truth 'Carrier Strike Group Two'. Thus did the NATO Striking Fleet role remain significant in secret war planning, although the primary official role of British carriers had been established in 1957 as limited war operations 'East of Suez'. Hence, when in 1965-66 the RAF was able to argue successfully that land-based air forces could carry out the East of Suez limited war roles more cost-effectively, Britain decided to give up her strike carriers. This was ironic as the old Norwegian Sea role that had saved the carriers in the early 1950s was already beginning to reassert itself.

The 1960s saw the Alliance move to a strategy of Flexible Response. This new concept emphasised the role of conventional forces both in crisis management and in taking a much larger share of

Below:
Another view of 'Strike Back'. The Royal Navy's Carrier Group 2 was not quite a full-scale striking group in 1957: 'Red Beard' nuclear bombs for British Fleet Air Arm Scimitars were still a year or two away. Nevertheless, the air and ASW cover provided by HMS *Ark Royal's* Sea Hawk and Sea Venom fighters, and Gannet ASW aircraft allowed the US carriers in Carrier Strike Group One greater concentration on their nuclear bombing missions. In principle things were not that different from the relationship of the ASW Striking Force and the Carrier Striking Force in today's Striking Fleet operations. The British fleet carrier is operating with the American heavy cruiser *Macon*. USNI

the deterrent burden especially on the flanks, both Northern and Southern. In 1963 Norway began to hold 'Cold Winter' exercises in northern Norway and the following year this was combined with the first Allied Command Europe (ACE) Mobile Force exercise in Norway, 'Northern Express'. Later, in 1964, the first 'Teamwork' exercise was held under SACLANT's command to practice the maritime reinforcement of Norway. The year 1965 saw Anglo-American participation in the 'Cold Winter' and Anglo-Norwegian anti-submarine exercises in the Norwegian Sea. 'Winter Express' was held with the AMF in 1966, establishing a biennial pattern that has been kept ever since, except for 1974.

In 1967, with the Alliance's overall deterrent strategy about to change, Rear-Adm Richard Colbert USN, Deputy Chief of Plans at SACLANT, called for a new concept of maritime strategy also. This would improve the Alliance's ability to respond quickly and collectively at sea in a crisis and would recognise the importance of the sea to the Alliance's overall strategy. With the new emphasis on crisis management, SACLANT's staff was evolving the concept of Maritime Contingency Forces to be drawn at short notice from assets earmarked to the Alliance in peacetime to support SACLANT's contingency plans at an early point in a crisis. As part of this process the Standing Naval Force Atlantic (SNFL) was born at the beginning of 1968 as a multi-national standing force under NATO command. This was approved at the same meeting of the

Flexible Response

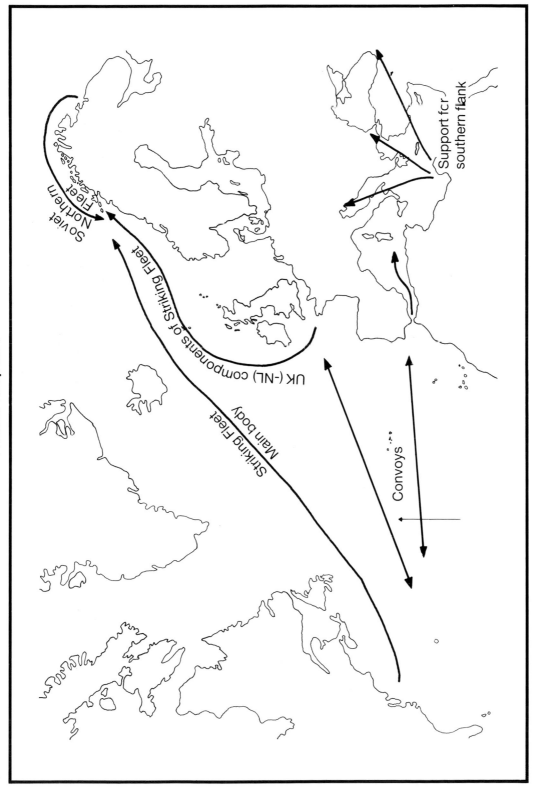

Soviet Northern Fleet

UK (-NL) components of Striking Fleet

Striking Fleet Main body

Support for southern flank

Convoys

NATO maritime exercises continued into the 1960s with the emphasis on massive nuclear strike co-existing somewhat uneasily with the continued exercising of ASW which implied a more protracted conflict. This dilemma was never resolved before NATO strategy evolved into 'Flexible Response' in 1967-68. The importance of joint operations with allied forces, however, remained strong. Here at Invergordon in 1961 is part of a NATO squadron composed of the Dutch ASW carrier *Karel Doorman* and three British 'Daring' class destroyers. *Karel Doorman* would find herself at war with the British 21 years later as the Argentine *25th of May*. USNI

Alliance's Defence Planning Committee at the end of 1967 that finally approved the formal abandonment of 'Massive Retaliation' and the adoption of Flexible Response. The Military Committee's new strategic document that enshrined the concept of 'Flexible Response', MC14/3, appeared at about the same time as SNFL. These were not the only epochal changes taking place at this time.

At the beginning of 1968 Britain also announced the imminent abandonment of her entire East of Suez presence, and to demonstrate the new orientation of her maritime forces sent the commando carrier HMS *Bulwark* to support the 'Polar Express' exercise in Norwegian waters, the largest exercise yet in the series.

Later in 1968 Colbert got his full investigation of Flexible Response's maritime implications when a special study was commissioned by NATO Secretary General Manlio Brosio. The Brosio study was carried out by members of the SACLANT staff and presented to the Secretary General in March 1969. It set out NATO's maritime strategy in tones that have a remarkably modern ring. In crisis, Maritime Contingency Forces would be mobilised to provide a controlled response and to deter further escalation. If, however, deterrence failed, Western maritime forces would be used to contain and destroy Soviet submarines as far forward as possible while strike

carriers would support the land and amphibious operations ashore, especially on the flanks. Defence of shipping would be concerted with an offensive against Soviet maritime forces.

The Brosio study played through a theoretical Norwegian scenario, postulating an invasion of northern Norway using amphibious and airborne forces. The Alliance used its warning time to bring carrier task forces into the Norwegian Sea, while anti-submarine barriers were set up in the Greenland-Iceland-Faeroes-UK (GIUK) gap and carrier and convoy escort units deployed in the Atlantic. When the shooting started the Allied carrier aircraft attacked the Soviet invaders ashore and were engaged in combat by Soviet naval aviation. Most Soviet submarines were held back for defensive purposes and the barriers and convoy escorts defeated the residual attack on shipping. The Allies were able to rotate sufficient carriers into the Norwegian Sea both to ensure the defeat of the attacks upon them and to allow the successful interdiction of the land invasion of Norway. The assessment was that after a three-month battle at sea using conventional weapons alone, the war would be won and the Soviets would be faced with the choice of accepting defeat or mounting a major attack on the Central Front.

At the Naval War College at Newport, war games began to be held under the name 'Establish Contact' in which a striking fleet of four American carriers and two British took on Soviet opposition in the Norwegian Sea. In the Norwegian Sea itself in September 1972 Exercise 'Strong Express' saw an Anglo-American carrier striking fleet support an amphibious reinforcement of the defence of northern Norway. Carrier Strike Group Two made up of HMS *Ark Royal* and an escorting Anglo-American force of cruisers, destroyers and frigates covered an Anglo-Dutch amphibious force which included HMS *Albion*, HMS *Fearless* and RFA *Sir Geraint* deployed in Norwegian waters to demonstrate the ability to reinforce if required. Forty-eight hours later Carrier Strike Group One, made up of the

USS *John F. Kennedy* and the rest of the Striking Fleet's amphibious component, complete with the command ship USS *Mount Whitney* arrived for, first, an unopposed deterrent landing and then a simulated opposed landing near Tromso. This was the first time US Marines had landed in northern Norway. The following year Exercise 'Swift Move' again saw the Striking Fleet exercising its ASW and air power projection capabilities in the Norwegian Sea.

The Brosio study had warned that although NATO could win a naval battle in 1968 the prospects for the future were less optimistic. Its authors feared that on

Below:
By 1964, although 'Flexible Response' was still a subject of debate at the highest levels in the Alliance, the new perceived importance of more limited crisis management operations led to their being exercised at sea and on the flanks. The first 'Teamwork' exercise took place that year to practice the maritime reinforcement of Norway. It lasted from 20 September to 2 October. The flagship of the Striking Fleet was the heavy cruiser *Newport News* (CA-148) seen here refuelling from the USS *Elokomin*. The large, guided-missile destroyers USS *Dewey* then confusingly classified by the USN as a 'frigate', (DLG-14) takes on fuel on the tanker's starboard side.

The Doubts of the 1970s

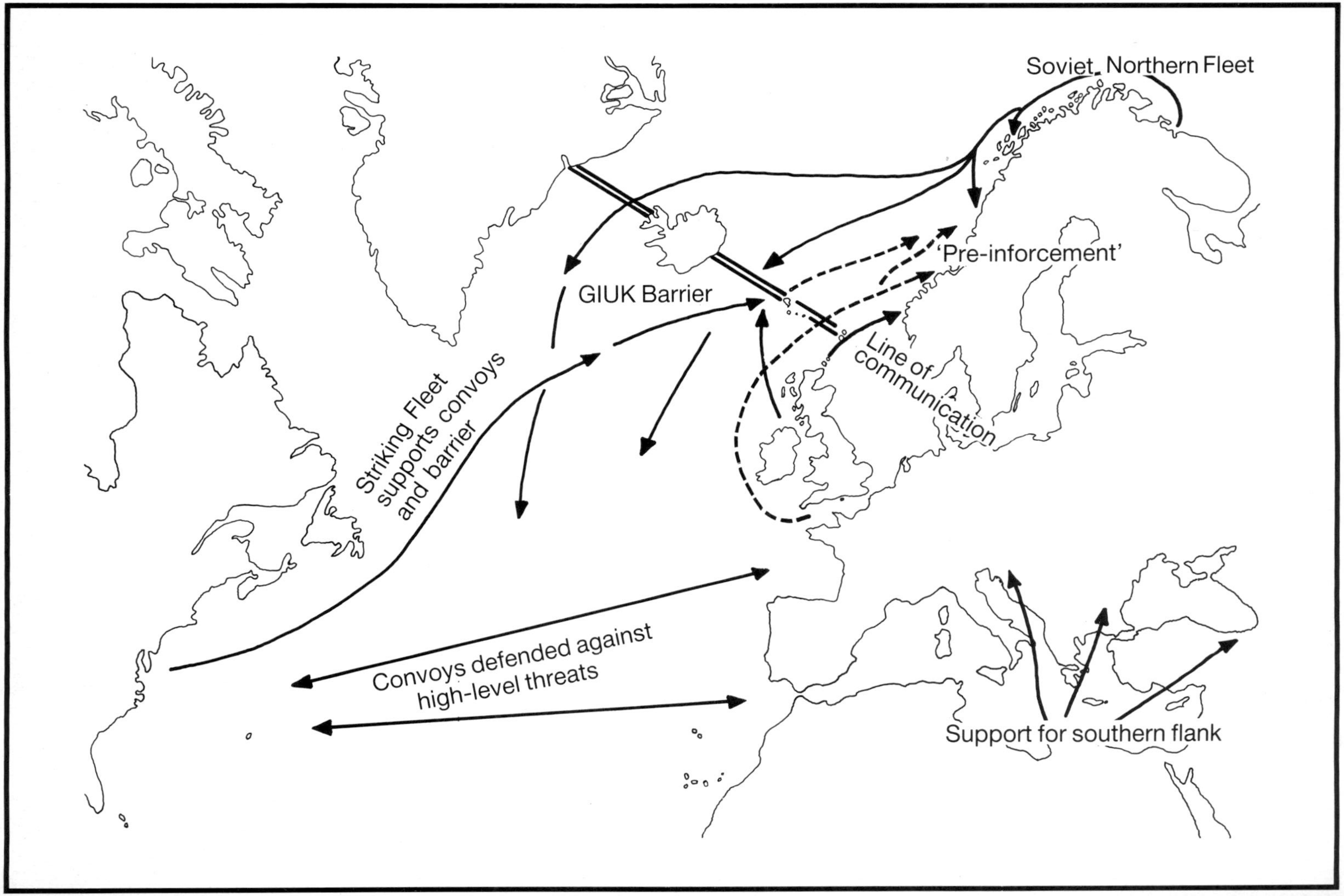

Soviet, Northern Fleet

'Pre-inforcement'

Line of communication

GIUK Barrier

Striking Fleet supports convoys and barrier

Convoys defended against high-level threats

Support for southern flank

then current trends, as Western maritime strength declined and Soviet strength increased, sea control in vital areas could no longer be assured by 1977. By this time NATO's traditional forward maritime strategy did seem to be in question. The problem was illustrated by Exercise 'Northern Wedding' held in September 1978. This was designed to practice the rapid reinforcement and resupply of Europe including the Northern Flank. However, Instead of actually entering the Norwegian Sea the Striking Fleet operated — in the words of the official publicity — to 'regain control' of the Shetlands transformed for exercise purposes into the mythical 'Normark' (representing southern Norway) and invaded by 'Orange' amphibious forces. The signals this scenario sent were decidedly mixed and the Norwegians, already disturbed by the post-Vietnam rundown of US carrier strength, began to get worried. Moreover, 'Northern Wedding' was the last time that a British strike carrier group operated with an American in a Northern Flank exercise. At the end of the year Britain paid off her last strike carrier, HMS *Ark Royal*, and reduced her main non-amphibious Striking Fleet role to the provision of Anti-Submarine Group Two, based around a light ASW carrier. Although the commitment to reinforce Norway in crisis and war still remained, barrier operations at the Greenland-Iceland-Faeroes-UK 'gap' rather than a forward carrier offensive, seemed to receive greater emphasis as the main comple-

ment to NATO's operations in the Atlantic itself. Even the Americans looked as if they might be moving away from their strike carrier strategy to build instead small 'sea control ships', small ASW carriers to engage Soviet submarines in the gaps and around the Atlantic convoys. This in turn reflected the development at the War College of new concepts of 'sea control' for limited time periods in limited areas that openly accepted that, in the era of the submarine and aircraft, old-fashioned command of the sea was unattainable. Even the ability of the Alliance to carry out amphibious operations against opposition began to be doubted at the highest level. Senior NATO naval commanders began to talk of 'pre-inforcement' before the shooting started rather than reinforcement against the full might of the Northern Fleet.

Below:
In 1964 the USN still had a force of ASW support carriers (CVS) of its own to give ASW cover to the Striking Fleet. This is USS *Wasp*, a rebuilt 'Essex' class fleet carrier operating during the first 'Teamwork'. She carries SH-2 ASW aircraft, SH-3 helicopters and AD Skyraiders (light strike aircraft). The disappearance of the American CVS force over the following decade was an important factor in causing NATO commanders to reassess their ability to move forward in a crisis. *USNI*

The Norwegians were not the only ones to be disturbed by the trend to place them on the wrong side of NATO's apparent defence perimeter. In 1977 NATO defence ministers had ordered a major reassessment of the Alliance's position at sea. There was a feeling that NATO's naval concepts were both ill-defined and too reactive. Western maritime strategy seemed in danger of becoming fixated with the 'Maginot Line' of the 'gap'. In 1978, successive SACLANTs, Admirals 'Ike' Kidd and Harry Train stressed the need for 'a balanced response' to Soviet naval forces in the Eastern Atlantic (EASTLANT) area and for NATO 'to be prepared and have the will to take full advantage of warning time and early action ... To place our striking force in positions to deter the enemy's combat fleet ...'. It was also felt that a more unified concept was required, especially where the three Major NATO Commands (MNCs) came together to control a common campaign.

Ministers therefore ordered the Alliance's military commanders and their staffs to draw up a broad statement of principles of how maritime forces should be used in support of the overall NATO strategic concept and its governing principles of deterrence, forward defence and flexible response. The result was the drafting by the three MNCs of the first edition of the Concept of Maritime Operations (CONMAROPS) that was drawn up in 1980 and approved by the Defence Planning Committee of the Alliance in 1981. This was a thorough assessment of the Alliance's maritime interests, the threats to those interests and the types of confrontation to be expected. Allied priorities in those confrontations were defined along with the roles of various kinds of forces in the five campaigns that were outlined: two in the Mediterranean with forces under SACEUR's command; two, Atlantic and Norwegian Sea, with forces under SACLANT; and one, Shallow Seas, with forces provided by SACLANT, SACEUR and CINCHAN.

As Vice-Adm Sir Geoffrey Dalton, Deputy Supreme Allied Commander Atlantic, told a conference arranged by the Norwegian Atlantic Committee in 1987, 'CONMAROPS establishes three oper-

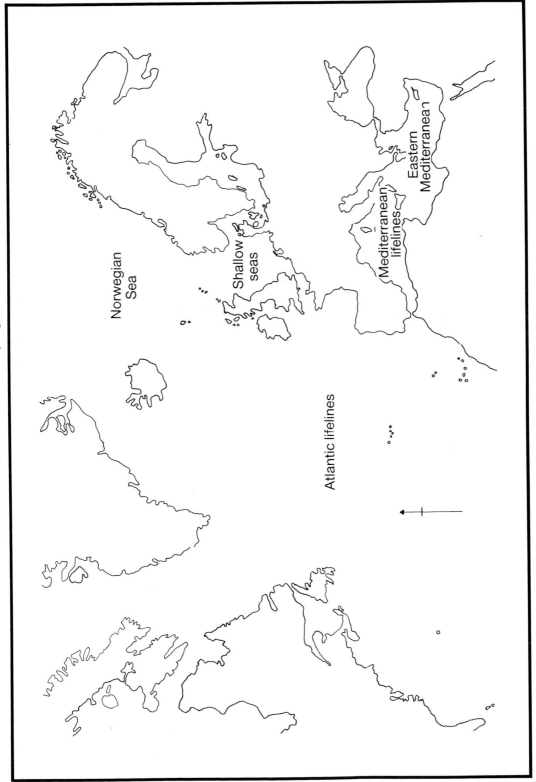

CONMAROPS Campaigns

Norwegian
Sea

Shallow
seas

Mediterranean
lifelines

Eastern
Mediterranean

Atlantic lifelines

ational principles: first — containment, keeping the Soviet fleet from reaching the open ocean either undetected in tension or unopposed in war; second — defence in depth, being ready to fight the Soviets at the forward edge of the NATO area, along their exit routes, and in defence of the Allied war and merchant shipping; and third — and most important — keeping the initiative.'

Using CONMAROPS as guidance the SACLANT Contingency Plans for use in times of tension were updated and revised in a Tri-MNC context, along with the General Defence Plans for use in wartime. The Contingency Plans, as before, have the aim of deterring hostilities by allowing the forces under SACLANT's command to be expanded beyond SNFL alone. These Contingency Plans are very flexible in the scale of forces they generate and when they may be applied. As tension increases, and each plan is approved by the DPC, more and more units would be transferred by nations to NATO control so that forces could be positioned to maximise their deterrent effect. SACLANT is helped greatly in this process by the fact that many of the Allied commanders involved are also national commanders: eg Commander Striking Fleet is Commander US Second Fleet, Commander Eastern Atlantic is the Royal Navy's CINCFLEET. These commanders can make anticipatory moves using national authority.

Above:
Just as in this year's exercise, emergencies occurred in Exercise 'Teamwork 64' that required rapid and unscheduled action. In 1964 a Dutch crewman's father fell seriously ill and the crewman had to be evacuated from the ASW carrier *Karel Doorman*. A British Fleet Air Arm Wessex HAS1 camouflaged for the East of Suez commando role but exercising in its secondary ASW capacity was diverted to fly the crewman to England. On the flightdeck can be seen one of *Karel Doorman's* Grumman S-2 Trackers, while a member of her ASW group, a Type 47 ASW destroyer, manoeuvres on the carrier's port side.

It was a sign of the times that in 'Teamwork 80' a carrier, the USS *Nimitz*, reappeared in Norwegian waters operating up to the latitude of Trondheim. The trend towards forward operations was, however, going further still. In March 1983, in hearings before the US House of Representatives' Armed Services Committee, the then SACLANT, Adm Wesley Macdonald, stated that the way to contain the majority of the Soviet forces was to take 'offensive actions that keep the Soviet Navy focused on threats to their own forces in the Norwegian and Barents Seas'. The distribution of forces at the outset of a conflict, he argued, was a vital factor in deciding whether this strategy could be carried out. The following year, before the same Committee, he returned to the need for NATO to 'be ready to carry the fight to the enemy and not to react to his actions, to deny him sanctuaries', and 'to threaten key elements of his warfighting strategy in his home waters'. Shortly after this statement Exercise 'Teamwork 84' saw the carrier USS *Independence* supporting the largest amphibious exercise in NATO's history and the first carried out in Arctic conditions. It involved 150 ships, 300 aircraft and 25,000 troops from seven countries and landings near Tromso. In an interview associated with this exercise, Adm Macdonald restated the need for early crisis deployment of NATO forces in the Norwegian Sea area, given Soviet strengths in the region.

Simultaneously with this Alliance effort, the United States was beginning a national re-assessment of its own maritime strategy. Adm Thomas B. Hayward was appointed Chief of Naval Operations (CNO) in 1978. In his previous appointment in the Pacific he had encouraged the development of a 'Sea Strike' concept based on the forward deployment of carrier forces against the periphery of the Soviet Union. On becoming CNO, Hayward brought this new and more offensive orientation to Washington. He also reorganised the Navy's machinery for strategic planning, notably the creation of annual Strategic Studies Groups housed at the Naval War College. In their initial work in 1981-83 the SSGs looked

specifically at the situation in Norway and adjacent waters and emphasised the need to capitalise on known Soviet missions and sensitivities. The traditional Soviet passion for home defence had acquired a new dimension in the 1970s with the appearance of Soviet ballistic missile firing submarines (SSBNs) with intercontinental ranged missiles that were deployed in defended 'bastions' close to the Soviet Union. Threatening both its homeland bases and the SSBN bastions might well contain the Northern Fleet and keep it away from the Atlantic. This implied forward deployment, something called for by the SSGs on more general grounds. They argued that if NATO's 'Forward Defence' concept was fully applied at sea in order to get forces

Below:
One of the core units of the Striking Fleet in 'Teamwork 64' was the attack carrier USS *Independence*. Wearing the classic markings of the period an F-4B Phantom fighter of VF84 is readied on the ship's steam catapult. These high endurance fighters maintained combat air patrols over the Striking Fleet's operational area then as the F-14 Tomcats do today. VF84 had recently re-equipped with the F-4B having previously operated F-8E Crusaders. In 1965 the carrier was in real action far away in Vietnam, a war which was to have a serious effect on NATO's maritime posture.
USNI

forward, their deterrent effect would be enhanced and they would be in the right place if deterrence failed.

The key event in the formulation of the US 'Maritime Strategy' was when Lt-Cdr Stan Weeks and Cdr Spencer Johnson of the US Navy's Strategic Concepts Branch in the Pentagon were tasked in 1982 with drafting a paper appraising how it was intended the US Navy was to be used in war. Adm Small, Vice-Chief of Naval Operations and a major exponent himself of the need for a new coherence and offensive mindedness in Navy thinking, wanted the paper to be an aid in programming and budgeting. Weeks integrated into a coherent whole the existing war plans of the US commanders-in-chief, including those of the US Atlantic Commander, Adm Train, NATO's SACLANT. Thus was existing thinking and planning, including NATO thinking, given a new coherence, emphasis and force. When presented with the Weeks-Johnson briefing in 1983, Adm Watkins, just appointed CNO, was enthusiastic; but articles were already appearing in the public domain criticising the apparent tension between 'Maritime Strategy and Coalition Defence'. The CNO therefore emphasised that the new statement should retain and even highlight its strong emphasis on co-operation with allies and the other services. The internal briefing document duly became the 'Maritime Strategy'

Above:
For strike purposes the *Independence* brought her three A-4 attack squadrons, one of which was VA-72 with A-4D aircraft. These were converting from their originally designed nuclear role to a more conventional purpose, as exercised in Norway. From the carrier they were vital air support assets for the amphibious landing and the initial overall land defence of the Northern area. If a real world crisis escalated, however, their capacity to range far afield (using in-flight refuelling) carrying awesome nuclear firepower, would come into play. NATO's official strategy still emphasised massive nuclear retaliation in any serious war scenario. *USNI*

which soon entered a second stage of development. The then Deputy CNO for Plans Policy and Operations, Rear-Adm Moreau, encouraged the new head of the Strategic Concepts Branch, Capt Roger Barnett and the replacement for the Weeks-Johnson team, Cdr Peter Swartz, to develop the thinking in the original paper into a broader statement of strategic priorities. Swartz continued Weeks' methodology of using as important sources current operational plans, including NATO defence plans. When their thinking was briefed back to them the American naval commanders-in-chief agreed that this was indeed what they had been about all along! The 'Maritime Strategy' was discussed in numerous classified briefings and continuously refined. It appeared as a classified document in 1984, was briefed to Congress in open hearings in 1985 and finally, after redrafting by the CNO's staff, an unclassified version was published over Adm Watkins' name at the beginning of 1986.

In this definitive form the 'Maritime Strategy' mapped out the US Navy's roles in peacetime, crisis and war. Forward deployments of forces were the key to success in all these contexts: Adm Watkins argued that in peace they signified interest and a willingness to stand by allies; in crisis they enhanced deterrence and controlled escalation; and in the event of war they allowed the initiative to be seized and the enemy to be put on the defensive. Once seized, the initiative was to be pressed home worldwide, with carrier battle groups rolling up the Soviets on the flanks and Western attack submarines inflicting attrition on SSBNs. This pressure would, it was hoped, achieve sufficient war termination leverage for the conflict to be concluded on terms favourable to the West before the nuclear threshold was crossed. All this was not too different from the logic of the Brosio study of almost two decades before.

As a national statement the Maritime Strategy was able to express, self-confidently and clearly, logical conclusions that it would have been difficult for NATO to have explored, especially in public. Nevertheless much of the thinking expressed in the American statement was an extension of the thought that had originally informed CONMAROPS. In fact the US Maritime Strategy and NATO Maritime Strategy were in full agreement with reference to the NATO area. When CONMAROPS was revised in 1985 and 1988 the American work helped confirm the emphasis on forward defence and seizing and maintaining the initiative. Moreover, in the mid 1980s the aggressively minded Striking Fleet commander, Vice-Adm Henry C. Mustin, experimented with new ways of operationally re-

Below:

In 1963-64, as the maritime implications of the flexible response debate were being thought through, Adm Sir Charles Madden, RN, NATO CINC Eastern Atlantic, proposed an extended exercise to be carried out by a small force of frigates of mixed nationality.

The force would take part in exercises, be trained jointly and demonstrate Alliance solidarity. In early 1965 Exercise 'Match Maker' began with four ships (left to right), the Royal Navy frigate *Leander,* **the Canadian destroyer escort** *Columbia,* **the Dutch ASW destroyer** *Overijssel* **and the escort ship** *Hammerberg* **from the USN. The success of this initial five-month deployment and two more similar exercises in 1966 and 1967 led to the conversion in 1968 of 'Matchmaker IV' into a permanent Standing Naval Force Atlantic (STANAVFORLANT, now more usually abbreviated to SNFL).** *USNI*

emphasising forward operations in the context both of CONMAROPS and the Maritime Strategy. Mustin took over in September 1984 and set about a major reorganisation of the Striking Fleet to create an integrated offensive whole; its Principal Subordinate Commands became Carrier Striking Force, ASW Striking Force, Amphibious Striking Force (the amphibious ships) and Marine Striking Force (the UK-Netherlands-US Marines). The Anti-Submarine Striking Force was the old Anti-Submarine Group Two, reborn as a multinational task force based around one or more British anti-submarine carriers and commanded by a British rear-admiral (Flag Officer Third Flotilla) with the job of keeping enemy submarines away from the American strike carriers and amphibious ships. National US Second Fleet organisation was aligned with that of the NATO Striking Fleet to allow more realistic training and easier transition to war, while much effort was put into tactical development by means of war games.

The fruits of this effort became apparent in Exercise 'Ocean Safari 85'. The 'Ocean Safari' series of exercises, begun in 1975, is designed to test the Alliance's ability to sail its vital shipping across the Atlantic in crisis and war. The two most recent exercises, in 1981 and 1983, had experimented with new forms of the direct protection of shipping, the controversial 'defended lanes'. The Striking Fleet had been deployed but in direct support of the

Above:
The North Atlantic Council approved of SNFL's creation in December 1967 and the first force began its operations in January 1968 with a British commander. Here is the initial group led by the ASW frigate HMS *Brighton*. There follows the Dutch ASW destroyer *Holland*, the Canadian destroyer escort *Gatineau*, the US destroyer *Holder* and a West German frigate *Koln*. The Norwegian destroyer escort *Oslo* was also a part of the original force. The officers who pressed for and obtained approval for SNFL were Rear-Adm Richard G. Colbert, Deputy Chief of Staff to Supreme Allied Commander Atlantic; SACLANT himself; Adm Thomas H. Moorer, his successor Adm E. P. Holmes; and Adm Sir John Frewen RN, Madden's successor at CINCEASTLANT. Colbert's intention that SNFL should be the basis for a larger formally constituted Maritime Contingency Force for mobilisation was not adopted, but in effect SNFL is a multinational contingency force in itself capable of early crisis deployment if required. *USNI*

defended shipping, eg in 1983 it had gone no further forward than the Bay of Biscay and Western Approaches. In 1985 the Striking Fleet was deployed in great strength, with three carriers and a battleship. At first these operated in a familiar way, in direct support of a convoy sailed from the East Coast of the United States. Two of the three carriers had to detach and the battleship continued with the convoy towards the Western Approaches. The carrier USS *America*, however, accompanied by Mustin flying his flag in the assault ship *Nassau*, continued through the GIUK with HMS *Illustrious* and ASW Striking Force under Royal Navy Rear-Adm Julian Oswald in the lead. USS *America* was inserted in Vestfiord, whose broad waters allowed sufficient sea room and whose geography and water conditions created a balance between the threat and the ability to counter it that could be exploited by the NATO forces. The carrier's aircraft operated in close co-operation with land-based air, American, British and Norwegian. This was a significant event in at least two ways. First, carrier air was being used forward without there necessarily being an amphibious landing to support. The aim was to use the forward deployed carrier as a major asset in winning the whole Atlantic battle. Secondly the fiords were being exploited for the first time as a key to winning the forward battle itself.

The fiord idea had at least two roots, one American and one British. It was first played out as early as 1978 at the US Naval War College. Because of the advantages of the option apparent from the war game, Capt R. Paul Ilg toured the fiords on Norwegian ferries to assess the practicality of carrier operations there. His positive report led directly to the first carrier fiord exercise. Also in March 1982, during Exercise 'Alloy Express' in northern Norway

the British Commodore Amphibious Warfare M. C. Clapp and his Flag Captain Jeremy Larken had experimented with putting their assault ship HMS *Fearless* in safe fiord havens protected by the mountains. Results were promising and the concept was combat-proven only a few weeks later in the Falklands when it was used to inform the decision to put the amphibious ships into San Carlos Water to protect them from the air-launched missile threat. This vindicated the 'fiord' thinking in an unexpected way and the Falklands experience created in turn the background for Mustin's development of the tactics

Below:
The first major NATO maritime exercise after the formal adoption of Flexible Response was Exercise 'Silver Tower' in September 1968. Significantly, with the new emphasis on the conventional aspects of deterrence, the exercise was the largest yet. The Americans made their displeasure felt at the forthcoming demise of the British carrier force. British ships were, however, not the only ones to disappear. This is the Canadian ASW carrier *Bonaventure* in the Firth of Forth taken from the US cruiser *Springfield*. *Bonaventure* had been given a final modernisation in 1966-67 but was paid off prematurely in 1970. The steady decline in major NATO naval units of the 1970s was to cast serious doubts over NATO's traditional forward maritime strategy. *USNI*

of fiord operations for the Striking Fleet's capital ships as well as amphibious units.

In 1986, the large Atlantic maritime exercise was 'Northern Wedding', a series held every four years since 1970 to practice reinforcement and support for SACEUR. The usual main emphasis in 'Northern Wedding' had been on the Central Front but in 1986 the exercise was considerably more 'northern' than its predecessors. As well as series of landings in Norway and Denmark, the exercise saw the Striking Fleet again explore the fiord option. Vice-Adm Larson, the new Striking Fleet commander, flew his flag in the *Mount Whitney* and brought across the carrier *Nimitz* and battleship *Iowa*; these had a close screen of two US cruisers, two US frigates and two Canadian destroyers and were supported by the ASW Striking Force based around Adm Oswald's flagship HMS *Ark Royal* and consisting of three British towed-array frigates, a Dutch and two American frigates. Again the big American carrier operated in Vestfiord. The pattern continued with 'Ocean Safari 87' — with some significant developments: a new departure was a pioneering 'freeplay' period in the GIUK to exercise tactics with the minimum of restraint. After this USS *Forrestal*, covered by HMS *Illustrious'* ASW force moved north into Vestfiord and, this time, Andfiord too, the furthest north a carrier had ever operated in Norwegian territorial waters. These forward oper-

Above:
The resurrection of a conventional rather than nuclear forward maritime strategy after the adoption of 'Flexible Response' by NATO in 1968 reached something of a peak in Exercise 'Strong Express' in September 1972. The initial move by an Anglo-Dutch amphibious force was covered by the British Carrier *Ark Royal* operating Buccaneer strike, Gannet AEW aircraft (seen here) and Phantom fighters. As the centrepiece of Carrier Striking Group 2 she continued to cover the landing operations in northern Norway together with the USS *John F. Kennedy* forming the other carrier group. The ability of a British carrier to provide local strike support to the initial deterrent move by European amphibious forces was as useful as the welcome support the British carrier gave after the Striking Fleet had concentrated. Everyone knew in 1972 that this capacity would not outlast the decade. *USAI*

ations, in turn, covered six convoys far to the south in the South Western Approaches to the UK and off Spain and Portugal.

What has been evolved over the last few years is a clear pattern of operating NATO's major fleet assets close inshore to the Norwegian coast. As Adm Larson made clear, both by his words and acts in 1987, there is no 'Vestfiord Strategy' but a strategy of forward defence requiring, if need be, the ability to operate and fight in and near the fiords. As stated above, exploiting geography gives the Striking Fleet a number of highly significant advantages. The high mountains of northern Norway give considerable cover from enemy sensors and make targets hard to find, let alone engage. Air attackers face the difficult choice of crossing Norway's well defended air space, not to mention that of neutral Sweden, or swinging the long way round North Cape, giving good warning and thus enhancing the defenders' chances of a successful outcome to the outer air battle. If enemy aircraft arrive over the mountains they have a near impossible task trying to find anything and are forced to search for high value targets creating multiple shooting opportunities for the defenders' missiles. Stand-off missile attack is even more difficult, if not impossible, and defending forces can be concentrated on any possible longer-range threat axes, eg against missile-launching bombers attempting shots up the length of the fiord from the open sea. Anti-submarine forces can also be concentrated around and off the fiord mouth to provide defence in depth against missile and long-range torpedo attack. Submarines would find it difficult to get past these defences and mining can also be utilised to protect the Striking Fleet in its bastion.

All the above depends on successful precursor operations by surface and air forces to clear the main fleet's operating area before it arrives. Finding enemy submarines against the jagged bottom contours, complex water movements and in the ever changing temperature and salinity gradients of the fiords is very difficult but the enemy submarine captain is probably even worse off. He has to use passive sonar as his only non-detectable sensor and, in the difficult conditions, this can rarely produce reliable enough information. He therefore has to use his periscope or some other mast and this greatly increases his chances of being attacked, either by the precursor forces or, if he survives that long, the close escort to the carrier battle group.

One can argue that going into the fiords allows the Striking Fleet commander to have a high degree of confidence that a fleet of three carrier battle groups,

Below:
In 'Strong Express' the Anglo-Dutch commando force poised itself for 48hr in Norwegian waters to demonstrate Alliance resolve before the US forces arrived and joined it for the deterrent and opposed landings. HMS *Albion* was the commando carrier (LPH) involved, seen operating in the fiords close to Tromso. Her air group is made up of Wessex 5s, although a Sea King is also visible. It was crucial for the Royal Navy and Royal Marines to emphasise their role on the NATO flanks after the withdrawal from East of Suez. *Albion* was paid off later in 1972 when she was replaced by the former strike carrier *Hermes* in the LPH role. This was the Suez veteran's last operational deployment. *USNI*

rather than four, will be sufficient to carry out the vital tasks of bottling up the Soviet Northern Fleet and creating such a threat to Soviet bases that the Northern Fleet's air and submarine assets will be drawn into a battle in which the NATO forces have all the inherent advantages of the defender. The fiord option is such a good one because it exploits all the advantages of the defensive form of war. Adm Mustin, its founder, would probably be shocked to realise this as he was always a prophet of the 'offensive'. Mustin very rightly insisted that his forces operated tactically with an offensive spirit at all times but at the operational and strategic level he tended to confuse the *initiative* with the offensive. Early forward movement into powerful *defensive* positions threatening the enemy's bases and communications — positions which the enemy ignores only at great peril and which he will thus be drawn into attacking under unfavourable conditions for himself — is, as Clausewitz long ago pointed out, a classic strategic manoeuvre with a long pedigree.

The actual forces available on the day cannot be predicted but whatever their size the exploitation of geography will allow the most to be made of them. This will create a considerable headache for the Commander of the Soviet Northern Fleet. He might consider at an early stage mining Norwegian coastal waters or sending quiet conventional submarines into the fiords to deny them to the carriers but this puts the ball of taking the escalatory initiative firmly back into the Soviet court. The Soviets, if they were indeed considering aggression, would thus be forced to show their hand at an early stage. Their forces would also be immediately exposed to attrition as crisis rules of engagement would allow attacks on potentially hostile submarines within sovereign territorial waters.

Using the leads coming up the Norwegian coast gives security for the fleet in the northern bastions to be built up as a crisis progresses. Even if three carriers were not immediately at hand, available

Below:
Asserting a role in Norway was vital to provide a continued rationale for the two British assault ships (LPDs) completed just as Britain was abandoning the 'East of Suez' role for which they were built. HMS *Fearless* is seen here docking down during 'Strong Express'. There was more to this than mere bureaucratic politics. The new requirement for conventional forces, especially on the flanks, made it fortunate that Britain had finally built such vessels in the 1960s for its then worldwide commitments. In the background can just be seen the stern of the third British amphibious unit deployed in 'Strong Express' the LSL *Sir Geraint*. 'Strong Express' in 1972 was the first time that US Marines joined their British counterparts in actually landing in Northern Norway. In 1982 *Fearless*, both in Norway and the Falklands, played a crucial role in developing the modern doctrine of operations in fiords as a protection from air and missile threats. *USNI*

assets could be brought in to begin the process of manipulating Soviet concerns, and providing extra strength in the whole Northern Norway area. The needs of immediate reinforcement and crisis response might require the very early deployment of European NATO naval forces and NATO's Standing Naval Force Atlantic (SNFL) both to bring in immediate land reinforcement and to begin precursor operations. Then some of these forces might fall back to help bring in the American carriers and amphibious forces. These might not immediately be of sufficient strength for war fighting, but even two American carriers would make an enormous difference in a crisis, not only in the hardware they would bring into the theatre but in the political interest they would signify. This multi-national naval presence would have enormous utility for crisis management purposes not least because it would not as yet pose an overwhelming offensive threat to the Soviets. Nevertheless the latter would have to worry about it and earmark assets to deal with it. Any surge deployment of submarines into the Atlantic would become a matter of risk while an early attack on the growing Striking Fleet would be deterred both by the risk of general war and NATO fleet's own strength in the defence, supported by shore-based forces and Norwegian geography. Another factor would also have to be borne in mind by the Soviets.

Above:

The core of Carrier Striking Group 1 during 'Strong Express' was the USS *John F. Kennedy*. Her F-4 Phantom fighters, A-6 Intruder and A-7 Corsair strike aircraft were a crucial addition to *Ark Royal's* air group, one of whose Buccaneers is engaged in a cross-decking exercise in the foreground. The picture symbolises the mix of British and US carrier air power that still underpinned NATO's forward operations in the North in the early 1970s. The presence of only one US carrier, however, reflected pressures of Vietnam deployments and the reduction of overall US carrier strength. *Ark Royal* was Britain's last strike carrier. Current war plans assumed four US and two British CVAs if the growing Northern fleet was to be defeated. Not for nothing were NATO's naval commanders worried and beginning to question their long-term ability to fight the Norwegian Sea battle. *USNI*

Even if they did wipe out the forces deployed early before the third carrier arrived, the escalatory effect of sinking two concentrated symbols of US power and prestige could be disastrous in terms of any attempt to win beneath the nuclear threshold.

At this point the crisis should wind down, but if it did not the Striking Fleet would be in good shape to begin its classical wartime battlefleet role. At the very least, its presence and latent striking power would tie down most of the Northern Fleet's offensive strength to defend the Soviet homeland should the Striking Fleet sortie on an offensive surge. The option of such a carrier offensive as far north as required has never been ruled out if certain conditions are fulfilled; eg if the Soviets did indeed send most of their naval forces out into the Atlantic to attack reinforcements and resupply shipping then they might have little left to protect themselves.

As, in crisis, the carriers took up positions in the fiords, further to the north the Anglo-American SSN force would be tying down the cream of Soviet naval strength, notably the finest Soviet SSNs, in a defensive ASW operation to preserve the Soviet SSBN force as a strategic reserve. When the quiet and deadly combats of the submariners began, Soviet anti-submarine ships and aircraft would provide extra ASW support. The Northern Fleet's aircraft-carrying cruisers and land-based aircraft would also keep NATO surface and air ASW forces at bay while the Soviet 'battlefleet', ie anti-surface warfare submarines and aircraft, might skirmish with the Striking Fleet. It would be in the traditions of classical maritime strategy for neither to push the battle to a conclusion as both these 'battlefleets' might achieve their functions more surely by being held as 'fleets in being', ie using the options each possessed to constrain the options of the other. And all the time the reinforcement ships might be arriving relatively unscathed.

Western carrier strike aircraft might prove disturbingly effective in their far-reaching activities in the north. They might be seen by Soviet commanders as the key to an unexpectedly spirited and successful defence of northern Norway. Alternatively, or additionally — together with TLAM-C cruise missile strikes from surface ships — they might be inflicting unacceptably heavy damage on Soviet facilities in the Kola and/or on the Soviet surface and carrier forces supporting the ASW battle in the SSBN bastions. The Striking Fleet's neutralisation might therefore seem imperative. Moreover the latent threat to the Kola from the Striking Fleet's nuclear bombs and missiles might also advise an attempt to destroy it to constrain at least one likely western nuclear first-use option. Most likely, perhaps the

Below:
The last 'Teamwork' in which a British attack carrier took part was the 1976 exercise, a large one involving 200 ships, 30 submarines and 300 aircraft. Here is *Ark Royal* being escorted by the large Dutch frigate *De Ruyter* with which she is making a jackstay transfer. It was still necessary to make such peacetime shows of strength on the Northern Flank but the real ability to reinforce in war was by then being seriously questioned. Without ships like *Ark Royal* capable of early deployment it seemed safer to 'pre-inforce' in crisis before the shouting started and then perhaps retreat to the Greenland-Iceland-UK gap to try to protect Atlantic communications with ships like *De Ruyter* supported by whatever carriers the Americans could bring up. *USNI*

By 1980 NATO's Concept of Maritime Operations (CONMAROPS) was re-emphasising the importance of both containment and defence in depth. Forward operations might be more than a peacetime demonstration after all, especially given Norwegian anxieties about the reliability of the Allied guarantee of reinforcement. This was again demonstrated in 'Teamwork 80'. Once again USMC forces were brought through the rough seas by America's impressive fleet of modern amphibious shipping, the ocean-going fast LST *Newport* (foreground) and the LPD USS *Ponce*. *USNI*

Soviets would grow frustrated at their inability to interdict shipping in the Atlantic because of their counter-deployments to neutralise the Striking Fleet's inconvenient presence in the fiords.

There might ensue a fleet action of a late-20th century kind with the Soviets throwing their submarines and their strike aircraft into the offensive. As the attackers, they would be vulnerable given the predictable threat axes provided by the terrain and the need to expose themselves to the layered anti-submarine, anti-air and anti-surface capabilities of the world's most sophisticated naval forces. They could not be sure of the outcome; only nuclear weapons would make success certain, but

nuclear use would undermine the whole Soviet concept of winning beneath the nuclear threshold. With each carrier supplementing its F-14s with its two squadrons of day attack F/A-18 aircraft in the fighter role, each carrier would have four fighter squadrons at its disposal and the Northern Fleet's anti-shipping striking forces might find themselves in serious trouble. Similarly, attacking submarines would be likely to give away their positions and thus invite their destruction. NATO losses could well be significant but the result of this fleet action might be to allow greater NATO pressure both on the bastions and the Kola. At this stage, after the initial engagement, some of the more ambitious options of exerting direct maritime pressure on the Soviet Union itself might become practical. It would be even more crucial for every Soviet maritime asset to be tasked with home defence.

It is in ways such as this that the Norwegian Sea battle contributes to the central NATO task of maintaining the ability of Western shipping to ply the Atlantic in crisis and war. If the Norwegian Sea battle is lost, possibly without a fight, then not only is a loyal ally forfeited to the other side but Soviet maritime forces are that much closer, not only to the vital Atlantic shipping but also to the United Kingdom and even the Central Front. The arguments

are therefore overwhelming for placing the Striking Fleet as far forward as prudence and the need to reinforce the land defenders dictate — probably, in the first instance, the Vestfiord/Andfiord area. This is not to say that the direct defence of Atlantic shipping can be neglected. There has been a disturbing tendency to view the Forward Strategy as some kind of alternative to operations in direct defence of shipping. This dangerously undermines the Forward Strategy itself because creating vulnerabilities further south — and there is nothing more vulnerable than unescorted shipping — would tempt the Soviets into containing the Striking Fleet and surging out sufficient submarines for a 'Happy Time' in the Atlantic and shallow seas. Only if the level of direct shipping defence is such as to require a substantial effort by the striking forces of the Northern Fleet, will Alliance forward operations be effective in diverting, containing and destroying the threat. As both CONMAROPS sets down and 'Ocean Safari 87' demonstrated, the forward operations of the Norwegian Sea Campaign and the convoys of the Atlantic Lifelines Campaign are integral parts of a synergistic whole. Equally, the forward operations

themselves require convoys to maintain their logistical 'tail'. There are no magic short cuts to success.

All this is but the late 20th century expression of the classical principles of maritime strategy as set down by Mahan and Corbett. There is thus nothing that is disturbingly new in substance, although the pre-1980s tendency for navies to be too reticent in reformulating and rearticulating their traditional doctrines gives a spurious air of novelty and, to critics, danger. The tendency for proponents and critics alike to concentrate on the war-fighting options in the Forward Maritime Strategy, that would only become practical relatively late in a conflict, has taken attention away from the more realistic parts of it relevant to crisis and the early days of a shooting war. So the time is right to take a look at what the Forward Strategy actually means in practice. There is no better way to do this than to examine the most recent full scale rehearsal of the Norwegian Sea Campaign, Exercise 'Teamwork 88'.

The Forward Strategy of the 1980s

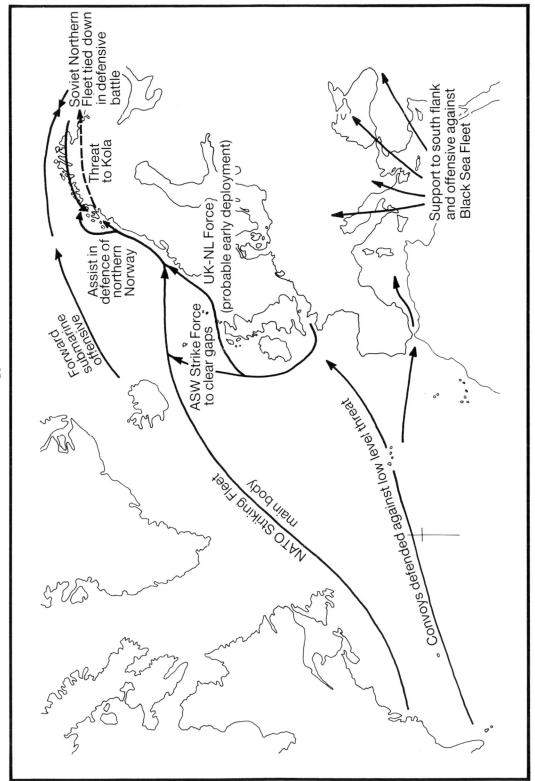

Soviet Northern Fleet tied down in defensive battle

Threat to Kola

Support to south flank and offensive against Black Sea Fleet

Assist in defence of northern Norway

UK-NL Force (probable early deployment)

Forward submarine offensive

ASW Strike Force to clear gaps

NATO Striking Fleet main body

Convoys defended against low level threat

2 Forces Gather

In the 1980s NATO's major maritime exercises followed a fixed pattern. Every other year there was an Atlantic shipping defence exercise 'Ocean Safari', held in 1981, 1983, 1985 and 1987. In the alternate years there was a Northern Flank exercise, alternately 'Northern Wedding' or 'Teamwork'. In 1988 it was 'Teamwork's' turn once more, although the decision was made to alter the pattern thereafter. 'Teamworks' were to be held on a biennial basis with alternate 'Ocean Safari' and 'Sharp Spear' (Shallow Seas) exercises. This change neatly corresponded with the change in emphasis in Alliance maritime strategy as 'Teamwork', concentrating on the Norwegian Sea, is the Forward Strategy rehearsal *par excellence*.

Major NATO exercises have one overriding aim: to demonstrate and improve the readiness of the Alliance's forces and headquarters in all maritime operations essential for the successful conduct of the campaigns set out in CONMAROPS. 'Teamwork 88' exercised the Norwegian Sea campaign. The main objectives of the exercise were to demonstrate both resolve and deterrence by the forward deployment of major NATO maritime forces into the Norwegian Sea.

'Teamwork' was meant to be a credible exercise in line with current strategy but clearly exercises are not the same as war and one must therefore be guarded in relating them to the real world. NATO provides both sides, which immediately shifts the performance of one side's weapons and platforms away from reality. In order to maximise training value, tasks and roles must be rotated, sometimes with little regard for operational logic. The forces actually engaged on both sides will be a great deal smaller than those which might be available in a real crisis. Other commitments, eg operational tasks in other parts of the world, must take precedence over 'war games', however vital the latter are. A notable example of this was 'Teamwork 90' which contained no US forces, absent because of the commitment in the Gulf.

The deterrent aim of the exercise is fulfilled by the mere presence of forces in the exercise area and the proof of their ability to operate there. It is probably the easiest objective to achieve. As for the other exercise objectives, these are inevitably tested in a somewhat rigid and stylised framework of pre-planned escalation. No matter what NATO or 'Blue' does, the other side, 'Orange', is going to resist in a preplanned way. This is exactly the opposite of the real world where, it is hoped, the forward deployment of NATO maritime forces would cause the Soviets to de-escalate. The need to test out both Contingency and General Defence Plans dictates the script.

Live exercises, however, have great training value which commanders wish to maximise with minimum pre-scripting. This has led to the creation of a whole different scenario, Grey versus Green for a 'Freeplay'

Below:
The flagship of the NATO Striking Fleet Atlantic, USS *Mount Whitney*. *Royal Dutch Navy*

The Carrier Striking Force

Top:
The impressive bulk of the nuclear powered carrier, USS *Theodore Roosevelt*, centrepiece of Carrier Striking Group 1. *Royal Dutch Navy*

Above:
USS *Comte de Grasse*, a 'Spruance' class destroyer, part of the *Theodore Roosevelt* carrier striking group. *USNI*

period lasting 96hr and superimposed on the overall Blue versus Orange scenario at the point the Striking Fleet approaches the Greenland-Iceland-UK (GIUK) Gap. Effectively at this point in the main 'crisis' scenario the latter is suspended and the NATO forces take up positions for an unscripted major battle between themselves. The aim is to provide a realistic environment for the evaluation of command and control arrangements and the practice of tactics. Each side assigns the other a Warsaw Pact identity and uses its Western capabilities in combat as if it was engaging real Soviet targets. Ammunition supplies are notionally limitless to encourage interaction in a tactical melée designed to hone tactical and operational skills of staffs ashore and afloat and to test out operational techniques in the closest approximation to real war an exercise can provide.

The main problem with Freeplay is that the strategic scenario is highly artificial. In 'Teamwork 88' the Striking Fleet, supported by forces based in Iceland and Norway, became Grey to oppose Green forces controlled by the Eastern Atlantic (EAST-LANT) and United Kingdom Air (UKAIR) commands controlled from Northwood. The latter should, of course, in the overall Orange versus Blue scenario have been helping insert the Striking Fleet into the

Norwegian Sea. This led to some dynamic, interesting, exciting and valuable combat (as described in the next chapter) but the threat axes and directions had little relation to reality. It is to be hoped that the NATO Striking Fleet never has to break through the GIUK Gap with the Soviets operating out of UK air bases!

In order to allow the two sides to separate without surveillance, a 'buffer zone' was established. The Striking Fleet was not allowed to carry out surveillance east of the buffer zone, EASTLANT and UKAIR were not allowed to reconnoitre west of the buffer zone. The definitions of what surveillance was actually allowed caused a little confusion in the event with different interpretations and opportunities for exercise gamesmanship. The latter is a problem in all exercise contexts as it is impossible, however hard one tries, to be entirely 'realistic' in one's actions.

Planning for a major exercise such as 'Teamwork' is a very long-term process. It begins within Allied Command Atlantic up to three years in advance with separate planners working on the proposed intelligence, warfare, plans, communications and operations aspects of the exercise. The proposals are then put to a tri-MNC committee which provides a 'shopping list' to nations of what it would like them to provide. The nations then come back with what they are willing to do and the exercise specification can be finally agreed. This takes about six months and leads to an initial planning conference which means that on the two-year current cycle one 'Teamwork' is

Above:
The USS *Charles F. Adams*, name ship of her class, contributed to the *Roosevelt* group's screen and also proved useful in an operational decoy (OPDEC) role. *USNI*

Above right:
The large guided-missile destroyer (DDG) *William V. Pratt* also formed part of the *Roosevelt* carrier group along with her sister ship *Mahan*. *USNI*

Right:
The *Roosevelt* group's screen had a 'Knox' class frigate, USS *Moinester*. *USNI*

being planned before the previous one has taken place. The first 'Teamwork 90' planning meeting took place in April 1988. At this conference, and the two subsequent major planning conferences, the various headquarters and nations involved engage in a process of give-and-take working out the detailed plans that are finally set out in a bulky 'Command Directive' finalised by the middle of the exercise year.

For all exercises an overall political scenario has to be drawn up to describe how the war between South (NATO) and North (WTO) begins. This is not intended to be a realistic prediction of the future. In fact it turns on its head the normal relationship of military action and political crisis. The crisis is provided as a

context for the planned military operations rather than vice versa. For 'Teamwork 88' the scenario ran as follows. In June 1988 relations between South (Blue) and North (Orange) began to deteriorate sharply: nuclear arms control negotiations became deadlocked. In the middle of July, North stepped up its propaganda campaign against South and threatened an arms build-up if South refused to make concessions in Geneva. The arms control talks did indeed break down and North closed its ports and airspace to South. Political concessions were made to North's Pact allies to enhance their solidarity. North began a logistical build-up with the conversion of factories to military production. Espionage and subversion increased, not least in Third World countries supplying strategic materials to the West. Leading Northern politicians began an intensive round of visits to Third World capitals as part of a diplomatic offensive. One item in the propaganda campaign was a NATO exercise planned for Norway and the Norwegian Sea. This was denounced as a 'provocation' by the North which put its naval forces on increased readiness and reinforced its northern airfields. More reconnaissance satellites were launched and the Norwegian Sea placed under continuous air surveillance. In mid-July NATO declared a state of 'Military Vigilance' and stepped up its surveillance of North, which in turn led North to state that it feared a pre-emptive attack on an important naval base.

At the beginning of August, therefore, North declared the Barents Sea a 'military exclusive zone':

all economic activities in the area could continue but only under North's control. The coastal population of northern Norway reacted with great concern and South protested strongly. Activation began of the Allied Maritime Contingency Plans to mobilise European naval forces. As these began to prepare themselves on 8 August North stated that South's deployments were unnecessarily large for defensive purposes. The general heightening of tension led to NATO going to 'Simple Alert' on the 10th and SACLANT initiating the contingency plans concerning US and Canadian forces on 12 August.

As the Striking Fleet and its Canadian Task Group prepared to move, Southern intelligence discovered on 21 August unusual communications and rear services activity in the North's Leningrad and Baltic military districts. On 23 August larger numbers of Northern intelligence-gathering units were noted passing into the Norwegian Sea and into the Atlantic.

Below:
The 'Adams' class destroyer Semmes helped screen the Forrestal group. *USNI*

Right:
The USS Pharris with her sister USS Elmer Montgomery helped provide ASW protection to the Forrestal group. *USNI*

Below right:
The ammunition ship Suribachi formed part of Carrier Striking Group 2. *USNI*

Three days later the Northern leader made a stinging and uncharacteristic verbal attack on Southern military precautions, stating that the North 'would take whatever action it considered suitable to redress any change in the balance of power'. These actions were already being taken. South's surveillance noted increased deployments of Northern submarines setting up a layered defence as far south as the GIUK Gap and unusually high Northern surveillance activities along the Norwegian coast. Large surface action groups were also working up in the Barents and Kara Seas covered by Northern aircraft. Northern airborne early warning and control aircraft (AWACS) were on constant patrol over the Kola Peninsula and amphibious roll on-roll off (ro-ro) shipping was beginning to concentrate at Pechenga. The ominous turn of events caused the DPC to approve the activation of the Contingency Plans covering the European NATO members' forces. These passed to NATO command on 29 August. At 12.00GMT on 31 August the exercise officially began (E-Day) and shortly afterwards the Contingency Plans covering the US and Canadian portions of the Striking Fleet were activated. On 30 August, Rear-Adm Hugo White's UK ASW Group had sailed from Plymouth to begin precursor operations on the GIUK Gap. On 1 September, SNFL left Antwerp to move towards the Gap, soon followed by the German and Dutch task groups.

The Dutch did indeed send a towed array frigate to join White's force but all three surface task groups had another part to play — that of the enemy in the Grey-Green scenario. The forces that had sailed from European ports were under EASTLANT's command at this stage (the Germans were in fact initially under Allied Command Europe's command as part of a Tri-MNC Contingency Plan) but on 5 September White's task group became a part of the Striking Fleet.

The time has now come to examine in more detail the forces so far described. The Striking Fleet Atlantic was commanded by Vice-Adm Jerome Johnson flying his flag in the command ship *Mount Whitney*. His Carrier Striking Force, commanded by Rear-Adm W. A. Dougherty, was composed of two carrier striking groups. One, was built around the nuclear-powered carrier *Theodore Roosevelt*, escorted by the nuclear-powered cruiser *South Carolina*, the Aegis cruiser *Leyte Gulf*, the 'Coontz' class destroyers *Mahan* and *William V. Pratt*, the 'Spruance' class destroyers *Moosbrugger* and *Comte De Grasse*, the 'Charles F. Adams' class destroyers *Charles F. Adams* and *Conyngham*, and the 'Knox' class frigate *Moinester*. It was supported by the fast combat support ship *Detroit*. The other carrier task group, which joined from the Mediterranean was based around the carrier *Forrestal* and escorted by the Aegis cruiser *Mobile Bay*, the

Below:
The replenishment oiler USS *Milwaukee* supported the *Forrestal* carrier striking group.

destroyer *Spruance*, name ship of her class and recently refitted with vertical launch cells for missiles, the 'Coontz' class destroyer *Dahlgren*, the 'Charles F. Adams' class destroyer *Semmes* and the 'Knox' class frigates *Elmer Montgomery* and *Pharris*. The replenishment oiler *Milwaukee* and ammunition ship *Suribachi* provided support.

The Amphibious Striking Force was composed of the helicopter assault ship (LHA) *Nassau* (flagship), the helicopter platform (LPH) *Inchon*, the landing ship dock *Portland* and the tank landing ships *Saginaw*, *La Moure County* and *Newport*. This shared escorts with the carriers and the pool of escorts was swelled by the Canadian Task Group under Cdre L. C. A. Westropp made up of the destroyer *Athabaskan*, the towed array frigates *Annapolis* and *Fraser*, the three other 'St Laurents', *Margaree*, *Ottawa* and *Saguenay* and the replenishment vessel *Preserver*.

The Canadians were earmarked to join the ASW Striking Force, commanded by British Rear-Adm Hugo White. This had sailed with the ASW carrier *Illustrious*, the towed array 'Leander' *Cleopatra*, the towed array Type 22s *Brave* and *Boxer* and the three RFAs *Resource*, *Olmeda* and *Gold Rover*.

ASW Striking Force is, however, a multi-national force and the British were joined by the Dutch towed

array frigate *Evertsen* and then by the two American towed array destroyers *Spruance* and *Moosbrugger*. The Canadians also assigned their pair of towed array ships to the main body of the force, but circumstances intervened and *Annapolis* had to make for Reykjavik to have her sonar repaired. This was not the only loss Adm White suffered before the action began. The collision in the Gulf which badly damaged HMS *Southampton* caused HMS *Boxer* to be sent back to the Gulf for Armilla Patrol duty, from which she had only just returned. *Boxer* had taken on board *Brave's* Lynx helicopter as the latter was carrying a Sea King and some rapid organisation saw the Lynx transferred to *Evertsen* before *Boxer* turned for home. Sadly, this interesting exercise in NATO interoperability was not rewarded as the helicopter developed a defect which could not be repaired. White's striking force was divided into two groups, the main body, clearing a path for the carriers against nuclear powered submarines in the deep water of the Iceland-Faeroes passage while the active sonar Canadians operated against diesel

submarines in the Faeroes-Shetland passage. Sadly *Saguinay* had to detach to Rosyth for repairs but for the Freeplay part of the exercise the Canadians were to be reinforced by HMS *Bristol*, HMS *Scylla* and the French destroyer *Tourville* from the covering force assigned to the UK-Netherlands amphibious group. Two American SSNs were assigned as associated support to the ASW Striking Force.

The Striking Fleet is a mighty air as well as naval force. *Theodore Roosevelt* was carrying 77 aircraft of Carrier Air Wing 8; 18 fighter interceptors; 18 all-weather attack aircraft; 18 fighter/day attack aircraft; eight S-3A Viking ASW aircraft; five EA-6B Prowler ECM aircraft; four E-2C Hawkeye AEW aircraft and six SH-3 Sea King ASW helicopters. *Forrestal* was carrying a rather differently structured air group of about the same size: two F-14 squadrons; two A-7 Corsair II attack squadrons; an A-6 squadron; an EA-6B squadron; an S-3A squadron; an E2C squadron and an SH-3 squadron. *Illustrious* was carrying eight Sea Harriers from 800 Squadron; three AEW Sea Kings from 849

Squadron, 11 Sea King ASW helicopters from 814 Squadron and a Sea King transport helicopter.

Land-based air support for the Striking Fleet at this stage came from Keflavik, Iceland and Oerland in Norway. The former base was deploying six F-15 fighters with KC-10/KC-135 tanker support and 12 maritime patrol aircraft (MPA), three Canadian Auroras and nine USN P-3Cs. Some of the P-3Cs were equipped with inverse synthetic aperture radar (ISAR) for over-the-horizon targeting; this advanced equipment can show the operator the shape of a contact. More P-3Cs — three American and three Dutch — were at Oerland, along with four E-3s of the multi-national NATO Airborne Early Warning force. The latter were intended to supplement the carrier-based AEW aircraft in compiling the air and surface pictures. B-52s flying from US bases had exercised with the Striking Fleet in the days after it sailed: four were then based at Fairford in Gloucestershire to operate with it against both naval and shore targets.

A large number of aircraft and aircraft types were allocated to 'Teamwork' flying from British bases. All but the B-52s were allocated to Green (the 'enemy' from the Striking Fleet's angle) for the next stage of the exercise. In addition to these, three German Atlantiques flying from Sola in southern Norway were part of Green's air assets.

Green had powerful surface and subsurface forces allocated to oppose the entry of the Striking Fleet (forces which it must be remembered would normally be helping the fleet on its way). Three surface action groups (SAGs) were available, the

Left:
The LPH *Inchon*. *USNI*

Below left:
The LPD *Portland*. *USNI*

Below:
The LST *Saginaw*. *USNI*

Above:
The LST *Newport*. *USNI*

Standing Naval Force Atlantic, the German Task Group and the Netherlands Task Group. The composition of these groups was as follows with the 'hostile' identity allocated by Grey in brackets.

Standing Naval Force Atlantic
USS *Hayler*, 'Spruance' class destroyer ('Moskva' class helicopter cruiser)

HNLMS *Abraham Crijnssen*, 'Kortenaer' class frigate ('Sovremenny' class destroyer)

HMCS *Gatineau*, Improved 'Restigouche' class frigate ('Koni' class frigate)

HMS *Penelope*, 'Leander' class frigate ('Krivak' class frigate)

FGS *Schleswig Holstein*, 'Hamburg' class destroyer ('Grisha' class frigate)

HNOMS *Trondheim*, 'Oslo' class frigate ('Kara' class cruiser)

BNS *Westhinder*, 'Wielengen' class frigate ('Riga' class frigate)

German Task Group
FGS *Rommel*, Modified 'Charles F. Adams' class destroyer (modified 'Kotlin' class destroyer)

FGS *Lutjens*, Modified 'Charles F. Adams' class destroyer (modified 'Kildin' class destroyer)

FGS *Bremen*, 'Bremen' class frigate ('Udaloy' class destroyer)

FGS *Emden*, 'Bremen' class frigate ('Udaloy' class destroyer)

FGS *Niedersachsen*, 'Bremen' class frigate ('Udaloy' class destroyer)

FGS *Karlsruhe*, 'Bremen' class frigate ('Udaloy' class destroyer)

FGS *Hessen*, 'Hamburg' class destroyer ('Kynda' class cruiser)

FGS *Lubeck*, 'Koln' class frigate (modified 'Kashin' class destroyer)

FGS *Rhon*, Type 704 replenishment tanker ('Dubna' class replenishment tanker)

FGS *Freiburg*, Type 701 support ship ('Andizhan' class naval cargo ship)

FGS *Spessart*, Type 704 replenishment tanker ('Kazbek' class replenishment tanker)

Netherlands Task Group
HNLMS *De Ruyter*, 'Tromp' class frigate ('Sverdlov' class cruiser)

HNLMS *Piet Heyn*, 'Kortenaer' class frigate ('Sovremenny' class destroyer)

HNLMS *Philips Van Almonde*, 'Kortenaer' class frigate ('Sovremenny' class destroyer)

HNLMS *Bloys Van Treslong*, 'Kortenaer' class frigate ('Sovremenny' class destroyer)

HNLMS *Poolster*, 'Poolster' class fast combat support ship ('Berezina' class replenishment ship)

Green had 10 submarines operating in a layered barrier. They were all Orange forces in the overall scenario. They were:

Nuclear submarines
USS *Narwhal* and HMS *Tireless* (westernmost barrier)

HMS *Splendid* and HMS *Torbay* (mid-barrier in deep water to west of the Faeroes)

Conventional submarines
Venus (French) and *U22* (W German) (shallower water closer to Faeroes)

HMS *Odin*, *U12* and *U21* (Shetland-Faeroes gap)

Zeehond (Dutch) (to the north of the Faeroes)

The exercise 'identities' of these boats were: *Narwhal* — 'Victor III' class; *Splendid* —

'Victor III' class; *Tireless* and *Torbay* — 'Charlie II' class; *Odin* — 'Foxtrot' class; *U12, 21* and *22* — 'Kilo' class; *Venus* — 'Foxtrot' class; *Zeehond* — 'Tango' class.

At 08.00 on 6 September Freeplay began. Grey's task was to assure the safe and timely arrival of the amphibious task group in Trondelag and to make two air strikes on Scotland. COMGREY was Adm Johnson at sea in *Mount Whitney*. In support of COMGREY, as his area shore headquarters, was the British Flag Officer Scotland and Northern Ireland, Vice-Adm Sir Jock Slater at Pitreavie wearing his NATO hat as COMNORLANT. This area HQ commanded the Oerland and Keflavik MPA and Fairford B-52s. It also liaised with the Grey submarine command in the submarine depot ship *L. Y. Spear*. The Iceland-based fighters, their tankers and the ISAR P-3 assets, were directly subordinate to COMGREY via the Iceland Island Command which also had direct liaison with COMAIR Grey, Adm Dougherty in the *Theodore Roosevelt*. The NATO AEW aircraft were directly subordinate to Dougherty alongside the two carrier air groups.

Johnson's plan was to delay entry into the Freeplay area with his main forces until a proper

The Canadian Task Group

Below:
Cdre Westropp's flagship, the destroyer *Athabaskan*. USNI

Bottom:
The towed array frigate *Annapolis*.

picture of the threat had been built up from his air and subsurface surveillance assets. Then Green could either be engaged or avoided. The task of Adm Oswald at Northwood (CINCEASTLANT) playing COMGREEN was to prevent Grey reaching his objective by attacking his mission essential units (MEUs), ie his major amphibious ships and carriers, with submarine, surface and air forces. The priority for his attacks were (a) amphibious shipping, (b) carriers, (c) the ASW Striking Force and (d) auxiliaries. In addition Green had to protect his land targets as if they were vital installations and to provide air cover for his surface action groups.

Of these three forces SNFL was in the lead as it had other vital duties to perform. It had to be in Vestfiord to begin ASW precursor operations for Blue by early on 10 September. Its task was, therefore, to engage the leading Grey elements, the ASW Striking Force, for which it waited in a barrier 100 miles west of the Faeroes, keeping as quiet as possible electronically. The Netherlands Task Group was moving southwest of the Faeroes to cover any early carrier air strikes on Green targets while the powerful German group was kept in reserve to the northwest. In order to try to build a surface picture, all Green MPA were being devoted to anti-surface warfare (ASUW) reconnaissance to the east of the buffer area. *Illustrious* with the ASW Striking Force was just inside this buffer zone building up an ASW picture. War was due to start at 08.00 on the 7th.

The Freeplay part of the exercise will form the subject of the next chapter. It will be treated in 'faction' form as if it was a 'real' NATO-WTO engagement. The geographical features will, however, be kept the same despite their obvious unreality. This may be salutary as the forces engaged are expending 'ammunition' without any regard for real supplies. This is, therefore, not a real engagement. Nevertheless, it is based on a foundation of what went on in the GIUK Gap in three busy days from 7 to 9 September 1988. One real-world strategic lesson may indeed be drawn from these rather artificial operational evolutions and interactions. Breaking into the Norwegian Sea against an opponent firmly ensconced in defensive positions would be an immensely difficult and expensive business. Early deployment of forces is, therefore, an essential feature of NATO's forward maritime strategy. Unless forces are deployed to Norwegian waters early they may never be able to get there at all.

Below:
Rear-Adm Hugo White's flagship *Illustrious*.
HMS Illustrious

Right:
One of ASWSTRIKFOR's most useful towed array assets, the exceptionally sharp-eared HMS *Cleopatra*, showing the 2031(I) equipment aft.
Ian Allan Library

Below right:
The Canadian towed array frigates attached themselves to White's command when available: this is *Fraser*.

Right:
Two American 'Spruance' class towed array destroyers also joined ASWSTRIKFOR — *Spruance* **and** *Moosbrugger* **(seen here).**

Top:
The supply ship RFA *Resource* **which supported ASWSTRIKFOR.** *Royal Navy*

Centre:
RFA *Olmeda* **was allocated to keep the ASW Striking Force topped up with fuel.** *Royal Navy*

Bottom:
USS *Jack* **one of the pair of submarines allocated to support ASWSTRIKFOR.** *USNI*

Left:
HMS *Bristol* was having an operational break from her usual training role. *Royal Navy*

Below:
The rebuilt Batch 3 'Leander' *Scylla*. *Royal Navy*

Bottom:
The large French frigate *Tourville*. *D&B Teague*

Right:
A Canadian Aurora maritime patrol aircraft. Together with US P-3s these were based in Iceland and proved vital assets in the ASW battle. *SACLANT*

Bottom right:
The exercise allowed NATO E-3 AEW aircraft to practice co-operation with NATO's naval forces. *Ian Allan Library*

Top left:
Flagship of the Dutch Task Group was the large and impressive Dutch frigate *De Ruyter*. *Naval Forces*

Bottom left:
USS *Narwhal* — part of the westernmost 'Green' barrier and in the event easily dealt with by 'Grey' forces — playing a 'Victor III'. *USNI*

Top:
HMS *Tireless* — a very hard submarine to find — playing a 'Charlie II'. *USNI*

Above left:
HMS *Splendid* — another difficult target — playing a 'Victor III' in the mid-barrier. *USNI*

Left:
***Torbay*, *Splendid's* companion in the mid-barrier, playing a 'Charlie II'.** *USEL*

Below:
The Dutch *Zeehond* playing a Soviet 'Tango', to be stationed north of the Faeroes. *Royal Dutch Navy*

Above:
Playing 'Kilos' were three German SSCs (coastal submarines) *U12*, *U21* and *U22*. This is *U22*.

Below:
The submarine depot ship USS *L. Y. Spear* was forward deployed as 'Grey' submarine command.

Bottom:
The *Theodore Roosevelt* slowly cruises eastwards as the transfer proceeds. Within two days she will be in simulated combat. *USNI*

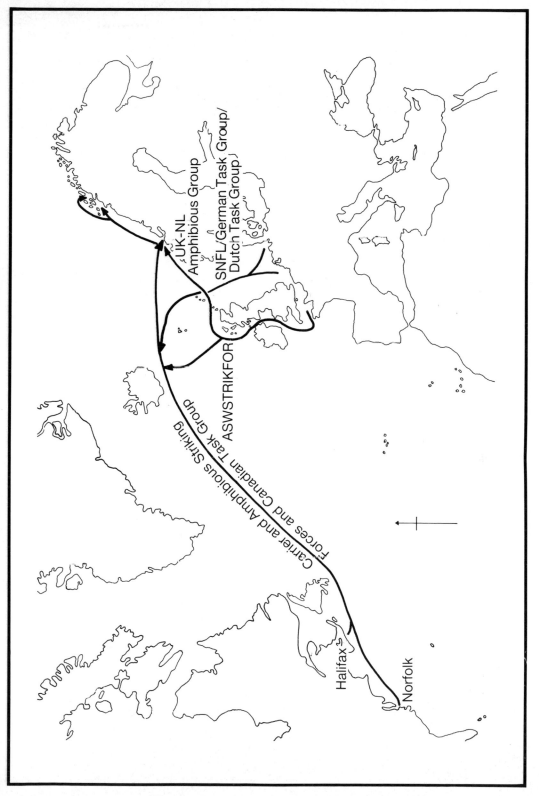

'Teamwork 88' — Schematic Movement of Forces

UK-NL Amphibious Group

SNFL/German Task Group/Dutch Task Group

ASWSTRIKFOR

Carrier and Amphibious Striking Forces and Canadian Task Group

Halifax

Norfolk

Above:
On 5 September, after the two carrier battle groups had met in mid-Atlantic, ammunition was transferred from the *Forrestal* to the *Theodore Roosevelt* by CH-46 Sea Knight helicopters of Helicopter Combat Support Squadron 6. *Forrestal*'s F-14 Tomcat fighters are in the foreground. *USNI*

Below:
As the Carrier Striking Fleet moved east its E-2C Hawkeye early warning aircraft maintained surveillance around the whole force. Here one of these vital AEW aircraft lands on the *Theodore Roosevelt*. *USNI*

3 The Battle for the Gaps

In the early evening of 6 September on board HMS *Illustrious*, the British rear-admiral commanding the ASW Striking Force was formally briefed on the current situation. The space allocated to the admiral's staff was crowded and tense. War seemed inevitable. ASW Striking Force was in her assigned position, well ahead of the main NATO Striking Fleet Atlantic and 200 miles to the south of Iceland. The Striking Fleet was composed of two CVBGs and an amphibious force aiming to land in the Trondelag area of southern Norway. But first the gauntlet of the Gap would have to be run and this was a much more daunting prospect than ever before. The daring enemy diplomacy that had prevailed upon newly independent Scotland to convert Kinloss and Lossiemouth into hostile air bases to 'defend the Norwegian Sea from aggressive NATO incursions' had helped spark off the crisis in the first place. Norway had resisted external pressure to do the same and now faced imminent invasion. The Striking Fleet was attempting to reinforce the beleaguered ally.

The admiral tried to look on the bright side. His ASW forces were performing splendidly. They were holding two contacts on their towed arrays. A 'Victor III' was being held at very long range by the towed arrays being trailed by HMS *Cleopatra* and HMCS *Fraser*. These were his rearmost ships and this 'Victor' was the closest known threat to the main forces. She would soon be dead, however, if the balloon did indeed go up. Even now a Canadian Aurora maritime patrol aircraft (MPA) was ready to pounce and S-3 anti-submarine aircraft were promised from the carrier battle groups. The rear-admiral's lead ship, the Dutch frigate *Evertsen*

Below:
The submarine *Baltimore* proved very useful to commander ASWSTRIKFOR in keeping contact with enemy submarines, although complete integration into the force proved impossible because of the problems of real-time communications with submarines. *USNI*

operating in the van with HMS *Brave* and the US submarine *Baltimore*, had a towed array contact on what sounded like another 'Victor III'. She kept contact as she sprinted and drifted eastwards. Between these vessels and the flagship were his two precious RFAs *Olmeda* and *Gold Rover*, whose refuelling schedule provided a full-time job for the RFA officer on the admiral's staff. Never was there a more frustrating task as tactical needs consistently took priority over logistical logic to ruin his best-laid plans. Between 'Lust' and 'Cleo', and slightly to the north, were *Spruance* and *Moosbrugger*, two big American destroyers only recently integrated with the force. The admiral would have liked to have met their captains, but the fog made unnecessary helicopter flying too dangerous. The fog was likely to clear in the early hours of the following morning, so the Met officer reported, but was likely to return. Fog was a two-edged asset: it made flying dangerous but it also made long-range target acquisition and engagement by the other side more difficult.

Above:
ASWSTRIKFOR's job was to prevent 'Charlie II' submarines like this closing the mission essential units (MEUs — carriers and amphibious ships). This was not an easy task and the submarine almost succeeded in sinking the carriers. *Naval Forces*

Below:
***Illustrious's* key weapons were her Sea Harriers but at the outset only four were available for combat air patrol (CAP) leaving another pair for probe missions. One of the major problems for the British carrier was the allocation of assets to CAP, probe and — when required — surface strike.** *HMS* Illustrious

Above right:
First victim of ASWSTRIKFOR was its own Dutch towed array frigate *Evertsen*, sunk in mistake for the *Abraham Crijnssen* of SNFL. *USNI*

What was the threat? Intelligence told him that there were three enemy surface action groups (SAGs) in the area. The lead one, coded SAG A, contained the large helicopter carrier *Moskva*. Possibly the most dangerous, however, was a group containing one of Baltic Sea Fleet's 'Kyndas': this

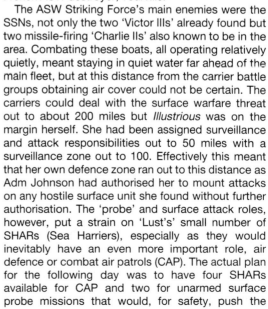

ship had been given as a priority target to *Baltimore*. As for the air threat, the enemy had moved a powerful striking force into newly acquired Lossie-mouth. Up to 24 Soviet Navy SU-24 'Fencers' were now based there along with a small number of 'Badger G' attack aircraft and 'Badger J' electronic warfare aircraft. Soviet fighters were also reported at other Scottish bases, not to mention tankers and airborne early warning aircraft. Two to three attacks, each of about 20 aircraft, were possible daily. These air forces were a particular threat to the Canadian ships tasked with the job of clearing the Faeroes-Shetland Gap from the diesel submarine threat. A 'Kilo' had already been spotted on the surface. The Canadians should have little problem in dealing with the submarines, he surmised, but their lack of AAW was a worry, especially so close to enemy bases. Thankfully, they would soon be reinforced by the Sea Dart-equipped destroyer HMS *Bristol*, the Sea Wolf-equipped frigate *Scylla*, as well as a large French ASW destroyer, *Tourville*.

The ASW Striking Force's main enemies were the SSNs, not only the two 'Victor IIIs' already found but two missile-firing 'Charlie IIs' also known to be in the area. Combating these boats, all operating relatively quietly, meant staying in quiet water far ahead of the main fleet, but at this distance from the carrier battle groups obtaining air cover could not be certain. The carriers could deal with the surface warfare threat out to about 200 miles but *Illustrious* was on the margin herself. She had been assigned surveillance and attack responsibilities out to 50 miles with a surveillance zone out to 100. Effectively this meant that her own defence zone ran out to this distance as Adm Johnson had authorised her to mount attacks on any hostile surface unit she found without further authorisation. The 'probe' and surface attack roles, however, put a strain on 'Lust's' small number of SHARs (Sea Harriers), especially as they would inevitably have an even more important role, air defence or combat air patrols (CAP). The actual plan for the following day was to have four SHARs available for CAP and two for unarmed surface probe missions that would, for safety, push the

surveillance zone out to 200 miles. It was the most that could be done.

At 08.00 the following morning the signal came, Norway had been invaded. It was war! There had been warning in the middle of the night, when serious jamming of the Striking Fleet's satellite communications had commenced. This meant that uniting the whole force into a unified whole would be extremely difficult. The commander of the ASW Strike Force would perhaps have been a little happier if he had known that his opponent had only a rough positional 'fix' on his flagship: only the frigates *Brave* and *Evertsen* had been positively identified by the enemy. He had used electronic intelligence 'Bears' to try to compile a picture, but to no avail. Luck, in fact, was not with the opposition as one key 'Bear' patrol aircraft could not maintain contact due to a radar malfunction. The planned initial enemy airstrike had, therefore, to be cancelled.

The Striking Fleet had been doing rather better in compiling a picture of the threats it was facing. The general location of both 'Charlie IIs' had been established by the ASW Striking Force, one boat to

the southwest and the other to the east, and this allowed Johnson to move his mission essential units (MEUs) to the north. An operational deception (OPDEC) group composed of destroyers emitting like carriers continued along to the south. ASW Striking Force had done its job perfectly so far and its AEW Sea Kings were also spelling the doom of the enemy surface units by rapidly compiling an accurate picture of the layout of the surface action groups, but then suddenly tragedy struck. As soon as war had been declared the unarmed 'probe' Sea Harriers were launched from the carrier and at 08.14 one reported a 'Sovremenny' at 25 miles in the vicinity of the frigate *Evertsen*. The latter, which had a contact in the correct spot, was told to engage with Harpoon. *Illustrious's* CAP SHARs with little 'trade' were re-roled with formidable Sea Eagle anti-surface missiles and were sent off after the contact. They found a target and, as the flagship was well within range of the 'Sovremenny's missiles, launched without positive identification. The Sea Eagles found their mark — and blew the poor *Evertsen* out of the water. The 'Sovremenny' had

Left:
USS *Hayler*, the 'enemy flagship', playing a 'Moskva' class helicopter cruiser photographed by the Sea Harrier that had set her ablaze with Sea Eagle missiles. She was later 'finished off' by US carrier aircraft after a 'missile engagement' with *Illustrious*. *HMS* Illustrious

Right:
What the Sea Harrier pilot actually saw as he flew by his target, HMS *Penelope* of SNFL. *HMS* Illustrious

Above:
What he imagined he was seeing: the 'Krivak' class frigate escorting *Moskva* about to be blown out of the water by missile attack. *Naval Forces*

been the Dutch vessel and the latter's target a neutral merchantman. Such is the fog of war.

As the tragedy began to dawn, the Striking Fleet took swift revenge on the westernmost 'Victor III'. The commander of ASW Striking Force knew it was vital to 'clobber' this threat as soon as possible. US P-3s and carrier-based S-3s carried out at least six repeated attacks, four and two respectively, and at 09.48 a large underwater explosion told its own story. *Evertsen* had been avenged.

Illustrious's Sea Harriers were also inflicting steady attrition on the leading surface action group. Three Sea Eagle-armed aircraft were launched, followed by two more about an hour later. The first sortie neutralised the closest sub-group of enemy

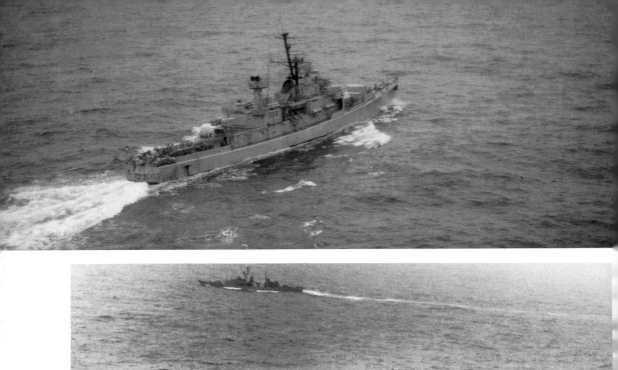

surface ships at about 08.45, setting *Moskva* ablaze and making short work of the 'Krivak' and the 'Riga' escorting her. One of *Moskva's* 'Hormone' helicopters, sent up for target acquisition purposes, was shot down by a Sea Dart from *Illustrious*. Another trio of enemy ships, the 'Sovremenny', a 'Kara' and a 'Grisha' were attacked by the second pair of SHARs, the 'Kara' being quickly set ablaze and left dead in the water. By 10.30 the surface threat had been effectively neutralised and less than 45min later the little 'Grisha', that had so far been left alone, was demolished by yet another Sea Eagle. Only the 'Sovremenny' remained, protected by the fog banks and the *Moskva*, bringing her fires under control.

Just before 11.00, after some initial difficulties, NATO early warning E-3s established a link with the ASW Striking Force, allowing the commander to use his AEW helicopters for surface search. Two more hostile SAGs coded B and C were somewhere ahead, one to the southeast and the other to the northeast respectively. The ASW Striking Force commander was concentrating his MPA and a pair of ISAR S-3s from the US carriers in this direction in search of the threat. He was also sending out his Sea Kings and Sea Harrier 'probes'. The US carriers were otherwise concentrating on the northeastern threat axis to unleash their awesome striking power on anything they found. For the time being the land-based air threat remained quiet with only a solitary 'Fencer' probe reported.

ASW Striking Force began to settle down in the late morning after the excitements of the previous few hours. A 'Charlie' class submarine was sniffed to the southwest and the Sea Harriers were regrouped once more for CAP as air raids were expected. Surface Action Group B now became an additional worry for ASW Striking Force but only one SHAR could be spared to probe for it. In order to increase his ASUW assets in the southwestern sector the commander, therefore, moved *Spruance*, carrying Tomahawk anti-ship missiles, to guard his southwestern flank. The MPA supporting his Canadians were carrying Harpoons and both the French destroyer and British frigate that had recently reinforced the Canadians were carrying Exocet. These would have to bear the brunt of any surface fighting.

Just as *Illustrious* prepared to launch her probe SHAR to look for the enemy, seven 'Fencers' suddenly appeared from the southwest, part of a larger strike of 12 'Fencers' and two 'Badger Gs' supported by seven 'Badger J' EW aircraft. There had been little warning as the relief AEW E-3 had not appeared, no AEW helicopters were available as immediate replacement and the carriers were still too far away to offer AEW or CAP support. The Soviet attackers were armed with AS-9 anti-radar missiles which had difficulty locking on to any targets. This meant that *Illustrious* was able to achieve copybook Sea Dart engagements on five of the attacking aircraft and a sixth ran into a wall of lead put up by the carrier's CIWS system. Only one missile scored a hit, but the damage was contained. It had been a close shave; with the right Soviet weapons the story might have been very different.

Now, however, another threat appeared. *Moskva's* damage control parties had managed to get her back into action and she closed for a showdown with *Illustrious*. A salvo of SA-N-3 missiles flashed from her missile rails and one hit *Illustrious* towards the stern causing a serious fire. *Illustrious*, however, was able to hit back and her Sea Darts were soon on their way. Two hits soon put the Soviet helicopter carrier out of action once more, although a US carrier air strike attempting to finish her off went astray and attacked USS *Spruance* instead; happily the mistake was noted before damage was done. A later US air strike had better luck and completed the destruction of SAG A. The 'Sovremenny' was hit repeatedly by Harpoon missiles and quickly sank. The Americans thought they were engaging SAG B, but in the event it did not matter.

The 'Fencers' were back late that afternoon with an escort of 'Flanker' long-range fighters but this

time the Sea Harriers, combined with F-14 and F-18 CAP provided by the US carriers, and the use of chaff to confuse the enemy prevented a serious threat developing. If the enemy air threat had been neutralised though, the submarines had not been. The estimated position of the remaining 'Victor III' was to the south of the force but suddenly a more accurate flaming datum of its position was obtained when at 17.17 HMS *Brave* was torpedoed. She slowly settled in the water as *Illustrious* and the rest of the group slowed so as not to be subject to

Left:
The Belgian frigate *Westhinder* — that was later to go aground in Vestfiord — in the role of a Soviet 'Riga' class frigate and under attack by a Royal Navy Sea Harrier early in the battle. *HMS* Illustrious

Centre left:
Rear-Adm Hugo White with his Flag Captain Jonathan Tod, are briefed with other officers on the developing battle. *HMS* Illustrious

Bottom left:
***Illustrious* forces her way through heavy seas. Both the Sea Dart launcher (left) and the Vulcan-Phalanx close-in weapons system (right) played a vital role in her survival against enemy air attack.** *HMS* Illustrious

Right:
A SHAR is launched on an unarmed probe mission. This major role of the Sea Harriers when both sides are keeping electronic emissions to a minimum must not be underestimated. *HMS* Illustrious

SS-N-9 attack from the two 'Charlies' also known to be in the area.

That evening the fog descended to symbolise the uncertainties in everyone's minds. Neither side was at all sure of the other's positions. A 'May' electronic intelligence aircraft did manage to get warning of the arrival of the Canadian ASW Group, now concentrating with *Bristol, Scylla* and *Tourville* in the Shetlands-Faeroes Gap, but there were no assets available to follow up the contact. The powerful 'Kynda'-based SAG C lurking to the north was a particular worry and the admiral and his flag captain discussed whether *Illustrious's* limited number of Sea Harriers should be concentrated to deal with it at dawn next morning. The choice was a difficult one. There were strong arguments for all the SHARs to be best left on CAP, given the inevitable slow

Below:
Personnel in *Illustrious's* operations room, dressed for combat, cope with the multi-dimensional threat. *HMS* Illustrious

Top left:
The 'Kynda' class cruiser and the Soviet surface action group it led caused COMASWSTRIKFOR considerable concern. *Naval Forces*

Centre left:
In reality this 'Kynda' group was played by the German Task Group, the destroyer *Lutjens* (left) was a 'modified Kildin' and frigate *Niedersachsen* (right) a 'Udaloy'.

Left:
Soviet 'Sovremenny' class destroyers proved troublesome. One disabled the Canadian frigate *Margaree*. *Naval Forces*

Above:
Once the 'Kynda'-led SAG was found it was rapidly engaged. *Spruance* launched Tomahawk anti-ship missiles in co-ordination with Harpoon missiles from *Moosbrugger* and P-3s. *USNI*

Top:
A 'Udaloy' burns after being hit in the stern by a Tomahawk missile from *Spruance*. *Naval Forces*

Above:
After coming close to sinking the amphibious force the modified 'Kashin' of SAG B was sunk by A-6 and A-7 strike aircraft from USS *Forrestal*. *Naval Forces*

speed of reaction in the provision of CAP from the US carrier force at a range of 200 miles. In the end, however, the admiral's view prevailed and all six SHARs were readied with Sea Eagles the following morning. The importance of organic air assets was being proved yet again. Also under consideration was the best way of routeing the carriers and amphibious ships which were now passing to the south of Iceland with the decoy group in the lead.

The *Roosevelt* battle group and the amphibious forces kept themselves as far north as possible. Another well established problem was also emerging: the correct distance in front of the carrier battle groups for the ASW Striking Fleet to be operating. Too close and the long-range passive detection capabilities of his force were degraded; too far and the provision of effective AAW and ASUW cover was almost impossible.

Late that night it looked as if the 'Kynda' group had been found. Nine contacts were spotted by air reconnaissance to the northeast of Iceland. An A-6 strike was immediately readied on the deck of the *Theodore Roosevelt* and ASW Striking Force prepared to co-ordinate a missile attack from *Moosbrugger* and *Spruance* with the 'war at sea' airstrike (WAS). The aircraft were 2min from their Harpoon launch points when an S-3 finally achieved

Throughout the battle *Illustrious* ASW Sea Kings kept up a constant sonar and radar search for enemy submarines. Four of the carrier's over-worked Sea Harriers are visible in the background.
HMS Illustrious

positive identification — on fishing boats. Quite literally at the last minute the A-6s turned back to the *Roosevelt* and the two destroyers stood their missile batteries down. The fishermen were probably unaware that anything untoward had occurred.

The powerful enemy SAG, therefore, remained an unknown quantity as the following morning, the 8th, dawned foggy and confusing. The confusion, of course, affected both sides as one enemy 'Kilo' put a torpedo into one of the 'Sovremennys' of Surface Action Group B. The conventional submarines were coming under pressure from the aggressively handled and skilled Canadians. HMCS *Athabaskan* managed to kill a 'Kilo', and the rest of the force dealt with two other boats. *Tourville* got an electronic fix on an indiscreet 'Sovremenny' but unfortunately was outside Exocet range so could not fire. Another 'Sovremenny' was luckier as she got a fix on HMCS

Margaree who she disabled with an SS-N-22 strike. The enemy submarine commander now regrouped his three available SSNs to concentrate on the Iceland-Faeroes Gap. The ASW Striking Force commander had little idea of where these enemy submarines were by this time and hoped to divert them with the decoy group as the carriers and amphibious ships slipped round on a northerly course and the *Forrestal* group moved rapidly south to carry out an air strike on the enemy installations being built up on the northwest tip of Scotland. An

early morning air strike had been planned but it had to be called off because of dense fog.

As the 'Charlies' moved quickly to their new positions they became vulnerable to detection and the Striking Fleet's most sensitive towed array frigate, HMS *Cleopatra* got a fleeting contact. Every available asset, two Sea Kings a P-3 and an S-3, was concentrated on the contact which faded as the submarine went quiet once more. The depleted ASW group received welcome reinforcement when HMCS *Annapolis* rejoined from Iceland after having had her towed array sonar repaired. The force was now spread out with *Spruance, Moosbrugger* and *Cleopatra* in the van, then *Illustrious* with *Annapolis* and *Fraser* bringing up the rear.

As the fog cleared that afternoon the surviving 'Fencers' attacked their primary target, the amphibious warfare group. The *Roosevelt's* fighters held

Left:
The Dutch frigate *De Ruyter*, a 'Sverdlov' class cruiser for the purposes of the exercise, is spotted by 'Grey' aircraft. After some success against the Grey forces she was 'damaged' by carrier air strikes and eventually 'sunk' by Harpoon missiles from P-3s and B-52s. *HMS* Illustrious

off the strike aircraft, while an escorting frigate attacked a suspected submarine contact. This turned out to be a 'NONSUB' but if the first 'Victor III' had not been sunk the previous day she would have been real enough. The clearer weather that had allowed the 'Fencers' to take off allowed *Forrestal* to get in a co-ordinated air strike on northwestern Scotland in the afternoon. The A-6s and F-18s were co-ordinated with a B-52 bomber attack and cruise missile salvos from the battle group's escorts. The B-52s were intercepted first and the defending fighters put up a major struggle. At 18.00 half a dozen 'Fencers' counterattacked the *Forrestal* group but their own jumpy fighter defences engaged them on the way out, causing the strike to be abandoned.

Now the balance of fortunes swung swiftly against the Striking Fleet. It had begun to break up into its

Below left:
As the 'Battle for the Gaps' proceeds on 8 September, *Forrestal* launches an A-7 air strike from her snow-covered decks. *USNI*

Below:
Steam rises from one of *Forrestal's* catapults as she prepares to launch an A-6E strike aircraft on 8 September. *USNI*

component parts. The USS *Theodore Roosevelt* prepared to dash south to relieve *Forrestal* as the strike carrier. This had the effect of helping the enemy submarines which had successfully evaded the ASW Striking Fleet and which could now more easily make interceptions against the dispersed targets. The surviving 'Victor III' carried out a series of attacks on the amphibious force, sinking a tank landing ship and disabling both *Nassau* and *Inchon*.

If this was not enough, one of the 'Charlie IIs' closed the carrier *Theodore Roosevelt* just as she became a perfect target, slowing in heavy weather to respot her flightdeck before she made her dash to the southeast. The 'Charlie' was tempted to make a torpedo, rather than missile, attack and lined up her six forward tubes. Just as the whole campaign hung in the balance the wheel of fortune lurched round one more. The cruiser *South Carolina*, the carrier's nuclear-powered close screen, appeared, her active sonar giving her a perfect fire control solution on the submarine. Before the 'Charlie' could fire, an Asroc ASW missile was in the air. The submarine had to evade but the Mk 46 torpedo scored a direct hit. The carrier lived to fight another day, but it had been a very close-run thing. The *Roosevelt* had come within an ace of being disabled, if not sunk.

The Striking Fleet's tenuous luck continued to hold into the evening. At 22.00 an ISAR P-3 from Iceland finally located the elusive 'Kynda' SAG. ASW Striking Force was within range for a co-ordinated Tomahawk and Harpoon strike from *Spruance* and *Moosbrugger* and P-3 maritime reconnaissance aircraft. The 'Kynda' and two of her escort 'Udaloys' were sunk, and the 'Dubna' class auxiliary was

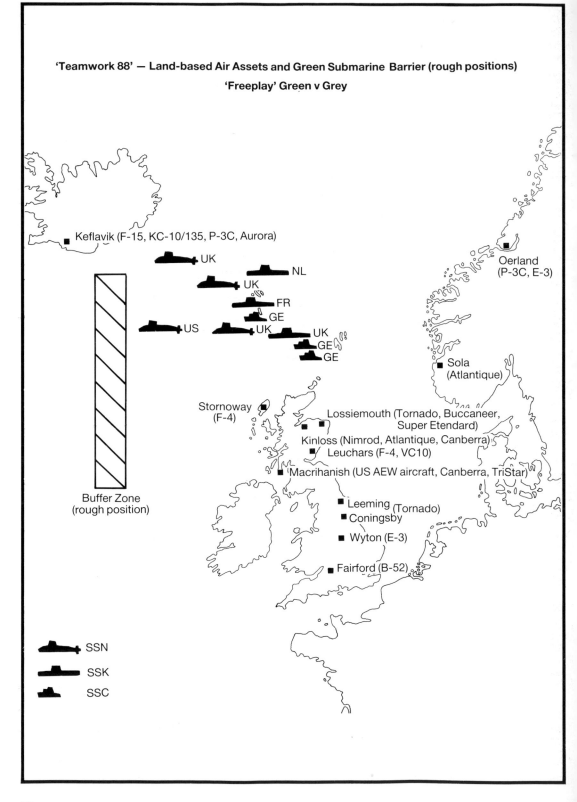

'Teamwork 88' — Land-based Air Assets and Green Submarine Barrier (rough positions)

'Freeplay' Green v Grey

Keflavik (F-15, KC-10/135, P-3C, Aurora)

UK

NL

UK

FR

GE

US

UK

UK

GE

GE

Oerland
(P-3C, E-3)

Sola
(Atlantique)

Stornoway
(F-4)

Lossiemouth (Tornado, Buccaneer,
Super Etendard)

Kinloss (Nimrod, Atlantique, Canberra)

Leuchars (F-4, VC10)

Macrihanish (US AEW aircraft, Canberra, TriStar)

Leeming (Tornado)

Coningsby

Wyton (E-3)

Fairford (B-52)

Buffer Zone
(rough position)

SSN

SSK

SSC

damaged. The rest of the force, a 'Kotlin' SAM, modified 'Kildin', modified 'Kashin' and pair of 'Udaloys', now moved south for a strike co-ordinated with SAG B on the crippled amphibians shortly before dawn on 9 September.

The latter group, made up of a 'Sverdlov' class cruiser and two surviving 'Sovremennys', had disappeared among the fishermen and the fog. It was obtaining little help in compiling a good picture of the 'enemy' from its air support but, nevertheless, was able to achieve a surprise attack on the amphibious ships. The aim was to finish off the cripples. In scenes reminiscent of a previous age of naval warfare the Soviet attackers traded missiles and then shells with the rakish destroyers *Dahlgren* and *Conyngham* and the frigate *Pharris*. The US ships sold their lives dearly to allow the torpedoed amphibians to effect repairs. *Nassau* only narrowly escaped being hit by an SS-N-22 that was decoyed away. Finally, like the cavalry coming over the hill, the *Forrestal's* A-7s and A-6s appeared to sink the modified 'Kashin' and drive the surviving, but wrecked, Soviet surface ships away. The damaged 'Dubna' had already been finished off by HMS *Scylla* using Sea Wolf missiles, while HMS *Bristol* found a 'Foxtrot' class submarine on the surface. The enemy boat dived but could not escape the Canadian dipping sonar Sea King called up to find and destroy it.

On ASW Striking Force's advice *Forrestal* was now moving through the Iceland-Faeroes passage well to the north of the line of conventional submarines expected in the shallow water north of the Faeroes. Meanwhile, the *Roosevelt* battle group fought out an equally climactic air battle with the Scottish land-based air. Every surviving 'Fencer', together with the 'Badger Gs' and the EW 'Badger Js', took on the F-14s and F-18s of the carrier. The depleted enemy air forces were no match for the battle group's defences and were shot out of the sky. Shortly after, the destruction of the enemy base complex around the old ranges at Tain was effected by *Roosevelt's* strike aircraft.

It looked as if the Striking Fleet had won a victory, confirmed as the wrecked survivors of SAG B were found and disabled by a Harpoon strike from P-3s and B-52s. The last engagement of the 8th was around the Faeroes as an enemy 'Tango' class submarine was sunk by a P-3. The NATO Striking Fleet's truly incredible luck had held. If the dice had been stacked another way, *Roosevelt* would have been a sinking wreck, *Illustrious* a burning hulk and the waters south of Iceland dotted with the wreckage of the amphibious task force. If the enemy had not kept his main air forces back to defend his home bases, the air threat might have proved even more dangerous. As it was the Striking Fleet's morale remained high as it entered the Norwegian Sea to come to Norway's rescue.

Postscript: The View from the Other Side

The above 'factionalised' account was the 'war' as seen by 'Grey'. But 'Green's' perspective was naturally somewhat different. Standing Naval Force Atlantic (SNFL) was the lead surface action group, coded SAG A by Grey. It only had 48hr of Freeplay, as it had to detach early to rejoin the main scenario in Vestfiord. Its 'war' went as follows:

SNFL was ordered by Northwood to establish itself as early as possible blocking the expected line of advance of the ASW Striking Force. Its commander, Rear-Adm John S. Redd, US Navy, planned to spread its units out just less than 20 miles apart. This would facilitate communication, help obtain easier cross-fixes on opponents and make it more difficult for Grey to obtain a good picture of SNFL's force deployment. It also allowed co-ordinated attacks to be made. The force was to keep a strict emission control regime until it began its attacks, relying on external sources, land-based aircraft, electronic listening and shore intelligence, to obtain a picture of the threat. The force's organic helicopters could clear up the picture within 100 miles of SNFL.

The main assigned target was HMS *Illustrious*, secondary targets being the rest of ASW Striking Force, both the escorts and the supply ships. Once Grey was localised an attack would be mounted, co-ordinated if time and distance permitted. In order best to exploit the range of its weapons, ships with helicopters and armed with Harpoon missiles, ie *Hayler* and *Crijnssen*, were to be placed at the northern and southern ends of the line. The two most powerful ASUW units, USS *Hayler* with Harpoon and HMS *Penelope* with a Sea Skua-armed Lynx helicopter, were both to be put to the northern end as this was *Illustrious's* most likely path.

At 02.00 on 6 September the force split into two surface action groups, A (SNFL's lettering), with *Hayler*, *Penelope* and the Belgian frigate *Westhinder* moved to carry out a helicopter pick-up of spare parts from Sumburgh and then went to its holding position west of the Faeroes. SAG B, *Abraham Crijnssen*, *Gatineau*, *Trondheim* and *Schleswig Holstein*, went directly to a holding position southwest of the Faeroes. At 08.00 on the 6th the force adopted radio silence, and by the early hours of the 7th all seven ships were in position using deceptive lighting to confuse the enemy. The destroyers and frigates variously masqueraded as merchant ships, cable layers and fishermen. Sadly, *Crijnssen*, upon whose radar-fitted Lynx and Harpoon missiles Adm Redd was relying as the southern anchor of his line, had to detach suddenly in the early hours of the 7th just before battle was due to commence to evacuate a sick crew member to Scotland.

As soon as Freeplay began, *Hayler* launched her SH-3 and *Penelope* her Lynx, the only radar-fitted helicopter left in the force. At 08.30 intelligence arrived as to the position of *Illustrious* just after 07.00 and at 08.35 one of the carrier's Sea Harriers was detected coming in from the west. *Hayler*, *Penelope* and *Westhinder* switched on their radars and engaged it. Sea Harrier attacks continued until 09.10 and 35min later *Penelope's* helicopter found *Illustrious* and attacked it with three simulated Sea Skua missiles. *Hayler* followed up with two Harpoon salvoes. The American destroyer's position was 72 miles from *Illustrious* and at half that distance she began to detect aircraft circling and IFF transmissions. There were other indications of the presence of a second carrier, probably the USS *Forrestal*, and *Hayler* launched Harpoon missiles at the expected position. In the event it was the marshalling point for *Illustrious's* Sea Harriers.

Penelope recovered and re-armed her Lynx, which was sent off to attack *Illustrious* once more at 11.21. This time it fired four simulated Sea Skua missiles. At 11.49 *Westhinder* and *Penelope* mounted a co-ordinated Exocet missile attack on the beleaguered British carrier. While this was going on *Hayler* took her 'enemy' sister ship *Moosbrugger* under 5in gunfire and at 13.25 HMS *Penelope* fired an Exocet at the USS *Spruance*. In the late afternoon SAG A began to come under pressure from the US carriers.

The two raids, one at 16.10 and another at 17.46, were repelled to SNFL's satisfaction, with an F-14 and an A-6 claimed shot down.

Meanwhile SAG B had been further subdivided by its Dutch commander into two groups. *Crijnssen* and *Schleswig Holstein* sped towards the sound of the guns, while *Gatineau* and *Trondheim* held position in case either the American carriers or the amphibious task group should appear. In the event the Dutch-German initiative was not rewarded and they arrived too late to contribute to the main action, but they did engage a suspected Canadian frigate en route.

Adm Redd had been frustrated by his lack of shore-based air surveillance which caused him great problems in compiling a surface picture. Communications difficulties prevented proper co-ordination with available assets. Nevertheless, Adm Redd was generally satisfied with his force's performance. To paraphrase his signalled report to Northwood:

'The force achieved the aim of missile attack on the carrier but the exercise yet again emphasised the value and utility of organic air. SNFL's aim of an early attack in the Freeplay was achieved in spite of sparse MPA, no CAP and lack of E-3A support. This said, however, and given the inherent artificialities of SNFL's employment, it was a most enjoyable exercise.'

Surface forces allocated to Orange for the exercise

Nationality	Vessel	Exercise Identity	Dates
Canada	*Margaree*	Modified 'Kildin' destroyer	15-18 Sept
France	*Tourville*	'Kresta 1' cruiser	15-18 Sept
Norway	Four Coastguard vessels	Intelligence gatherers (AGIs)	10-16 Sept
Norway	*Rauk, Hauk, Kiapp* and *Falk*	'Osa' class missile boats	10-18 Sept
Netherlands	*De Ruyter*	'Kirov' class cruiser	17-20 Sept
Netherlands	*Piet Heyn, Philips Van Almonde, Bloys Van Treslong*	'Sovremenny' class destroyers	17-20 Sept
Netherlands	*Poolster*	'Berezina' class oiler	17-20 Sept
FGR	*Hessen*	Modified 'Kashin' destroyer	12-18 Sept
FGR	*Lubeck*	'Slava' class cruiser	12-18 Sept
FGR	*Harz*	'Kazbeck' class oiler	12-18 Sept

The submarines were as allocated to Green for the Freeplay plus three little 370-ton Norwegian boats, *Kinn, Utstein* and *Kaura*, playing 'Foxtrots' from 10-21 September. It might be added that these three German-built Type 207s were much more difficult to find than genuine 'Foxtrot' class submarines.

4 The Striking Fleet Approaches

Rear-Adm Redd had to disengage his forces from the Battle for the Gaps at 08.00 on 8 September because he had pressing and vital business elsewhere. Together with the Canadian Task Group, his squadron had the job of preparing Vestfiord to accept the carrier battle groups. It has to be accepted that the Soviets would try to prevent, or interfere with, access by the Striking Fleet to its fiord 'safe haven'. They have two major means of doing this relatively covertly at an early stage of crisis, by mining the fiord approaches using aircraft, merchant ships and submarines and by the emplacement of quiet conventional submarines. To counter these threats precursor operations are essential, to deal with any mines and to neutralise and, if possible, to kill the submarines. Defensive mining can also be employed to keep at bay enemy submarines.

The main task of clearing mines from Vestfiord was given to NATO's Standing Naval Force Channel (STANAVFORCHAN) reinforced by extra British units. The force was composed as follows:

Mosel (flag) Federal German 'Rhein' class mine countermeasures support ship
Marburg Federal German Type 331B coastal minehunter
Breydel Belgian ex-US 'Aggressive' class minehunter/sweeper
Schiedam Dutch 'Tripartite' class coastal mine-hunter/sweeper
Ledbury British 'Hunt' class minehunter/sweeper
Sheraton British 'Ton' class coastal minehunter/sweeper
Kvina Norwegian ex-US 'Falcon' class coastal minesweeper

Below:
The primary task of dealing with the mine threat in the fiords was given to STANAVFORCHAN, here seen in Norwegian waters. The lack of variable depth mine-hunting sonars was a real problem in dealing with mines in the difficult fiord conditions. *NATO*

The extra reinforcements were the 'Hunt' class minehunter/sweepers *Brecon* and *Bicester*.

The Vestfiord mine countermeasures operations that began on 5 September demonstrated the problems posed by the perennial neglect of mine counter-measures by NATO's navies. First, the allocated assets would almost certainly have pressing duties elsewhere in Channel Command. Moreover, STAN-AVFORCHAN is primarily a shallow water force. Its modern minehunters can easily cope with its home

Left:
Two 'Brecon' class minehunters reinforced STANAVFORCHAN for fiord MCM precursor operations. They were *Brecon* (seen here) and *Bicester*. *Naval Forces*

Below:
A major real threat in case of war in the fiords would be modern Soviet 'Kilo' class submarines. The aim of the ASW precursor operations is to destroy or pin down such threats allowing the carriers safely to insert themselves in their bastions. *Naval Forces*

Bottom:
USS *Hayler*, newest destroyer in the US Navy and flagship of SNFL. For days on end she used her powerful active and passive sonar to plumb the depths of Vestfiord.

waters with their excellent hull sonars but the deep, difficult waters of the fiords are not suitable for such sensors. Only *Breydel* had the necessary variable depth sonar capability but this old ship had serviceability problems and was little help. Both variable depth sonar and advanced deep sweeping gear are vital and urgent requirements if the fiord strategy is not to be quite literally undermined. Four British 'River' class 'extra deep armed team sweep' fleet minesweepers (MSFs) were originally allocated to 'Teamwork' operations off Vestfiord, along with four Norwegian 'craft of opportunity' converted to the minesweeping role. In the event these plans were changed (the British MSFs were used in the Clyde area) but such assets are crucial to the viability of the forward strategy. Norway at least has noted the need and is investing in deep-water mine counter-measures. The new British 'Sandown' class single-role minehunters will also have a variable depth sonar that will be very useful in future fiord operations.

On 7 September, USAF B-52s laid exercise mines to prevent the entry of enemy submarines to Vestfiord and by 10 September both SNFL and the Canadian Task Group were in position for their ASW operations in the Vestfiord. Approaching the fiord *Penelope* and *Schleswig Holstein* had 'used' guns to fight off an attack by Orange FPBs which were jumping the gun somewhat as 'war' had not yet started. The Canadian commander, Cdre Charles Westropp, was in command of the combined ASW group, under the overall authority of the North Norwegian Shore Command (COMNON) Vice-Adm Torolf Rein at Reitan near Bodo.

The aim of the ASW precursor operation was to neutralise the enemy submarine threat in the Vestfiord. Together with maritime patrol aircraft, the ASW surface ships patrolled and the fiord in a systematic way using their radar and sonar sensors not only to look for contacts but to force the submarines to stay quiet, still and pinned down. The latter is vitally important as actually finding submarines in fiord waters is exceptionally difficult. The mixed watermass of salt and fresh water, the rocky sea bottom conditions and the complex water movements lead to many false echoes and very low sonar ranges, even for low-frequency active sets. The latter can sometimes get a good long-range path that suddenly might increase detection range by a factor of 10, but such performances cannot be relied upon. Against quiet conventional submarines running on batteries passive sonar is of little use and even when the submarines use their diesels and snorkels the large number of fishing boats mask the sound. The most effective sonars for use in fiord conditions are dipping sonars from helicopters and variable depth sonar in surface ships: both have the flexibility to be used at optimum depth depending on the ever-changing conditions. The Dutch decision to

outfit their Lynx helicopters with French DUAV 4 dipping sonar with its good performance in conditions of high reverberation has been vindicated by the requirements of fiord operations: *Abraham Crijnssen's* Lynx was a great ASW asset, with similar sonar performance in these conditions to a big Sea King. Sadly, *Hayler's* SH-3 was unserviceable with a gearbox defect but Canadian AQS-13-equipped Sea King helicopters were carried by HMCS *Athabaskan, Margaree* and *Saguenay* (returned from her Rosyth repairs). The same three ships also carry variable depth sonar, a low-frequency SQS-505 in *Athabaskan* and medium frequency SQS-504 in the other two. SNFL had two VDS ships, HMCS *Gatineau* (SQS-505) and the Norwegian frigate *Trondheim* (French designed Spherion system). *Hayler* was the only towed array ship, and a towed array like a VDS can be trailed at the optimum depth for the conditions. Nevertheless, fiords hardly offer the best passive detection conditions: on the whole SNFL's flagship stayed towards the mouth of the fiord where her array could get a good 'view' both up it and out to sea. Aptly, her captain was none other than Cdr Stan Weeks, the officer responsible for the original draft of the Maritime Strategy six years before: now he was putting his ideas into practice. The available assets were formed into four surface action units (SAUs): A — *Athabaskan, Westhinder* and *Saguenay*; B — *Hayler* and *Gatineau*; C — *Crijnssen, Trondheim* and *Penelope*; D — *Schleswig Holstein* and *Margaree*. These were then allocated search areas which varied over time. The force's helicopters would be given a section of their own.

HMCS *Preserver* moved around the patrol areas providing fuel to the entire force but shortly after 06.30 on the morning of the 11th disaster struck. HMS *Penelope* came alongside the Canadian auxiliary that was already refuelling *Trondheim* but the British frigate swung across *Preserver's* bows. Thanks to quick thinking in *Preserver*, *Trondheim* broke away and the big tanker turned away to port. This mitigated the effects of the inevitable collision but the strongly-built Canadian ship tore a 20ft gash down the frigate's side amidships, caused some underwater damage, toppled a satellite communications antenna and demolished a chaff rocket launcher. The frigate was quite seriously damaged and had to withdraw. Happily, the huge destroyer tender USS *Puget Sound* had been forward deployed to Norway as an experiment in afloat support of forward operations and she was able to rendezvous with *Penelope* north of the island of Landegode and do a remarkable patching job before the sad *Penelope* sailed for home and more extensive repairs.

Puget Sound was to get more trade on the 13th. Norwegian coastal waters are notoriously difficult given the large number of rocky pinnacles. During World War 2 the British cruiser *Effingham* had been

lost on one and German warships often had to abort operations because of groundings, notably in the PQ17 operation when the pocket battleship *Lützow* and five destroyers went aground in the Vestfiord area. SNFL had operated in these waters before quite safely but just before 14.45 the Belgian frigate *Westhinder*, operating too close to the southern shore in her enthusiasm to find lurking submarines, hit a rock on the south end of Kjengboen. The engine room was holed. The flagship *Athabaskan* was naturally anxious to help but in her haste touched the rock herself, damaging her sonar dome and some plating. *Puget Sound* sent a damage assessment team to *Westhinder* and again was able to patch her up. The unlucky little Belgian frigate suffered further superficial damage when the weather worsened as she was moored alongside the depot ship. *Westhinder* eventually put into Bodø where she was later joined by *Athabaskan*.

It was all a salutary lesson in the hazards of operating in these dangerous waters, but as some compensation the precursor operations were more successful in dealing with the submarine threat than ever before. Cdre Westropp's forces effectively won the battle for Vestfiord. The Orange submarines were kept under the constant pressure of surface ship sonar, radar and visual searches. Maritime patrol aircraft were constantly flying over probing the fiord for radar and visual detections, and magnetic anomaly detector surveillance and dipping sonar helicopters were engaging in continuous searches. This made it hazardous for submarines to come shallow to recharge their batteries, clarify their acoustic picture or even find out precisely where they were. The difficult water conditions cut both ways. When enemy submarines did pop their masts above the water they were vulnerable to visual lookouts and radar, expecially those in the air. Maritime patrol aircraft were responsible for the two confirmed submarine kills, but the victories were due to the whole anti-submarine warfare (ASW) team. Inevitably only a small fraction of the submarine contacts turned out to be real and weapons were held back for the most certain. Only once were they wasted on a spurious echo, on six other occasions when attacks were carried out a real target existed. This was a tremendous improvement on earlier experience and a potent demonstration of both the effectiveness of NATO forces in a fiord environment

Above:
The Canadian auxiliary *Preserver* kept SNFL and the Canadian ships supplied during precursor operations in Vestfiord. Sadly she was involved in a serious collision with the British frigate *Penelope* that caused the latter to withdraw from the exercise. *SACLANT*

and the value of realistic exercises, even if a price eventually has to be paid for the realism. By the time the main Striking Fleet appeared on 14 September the inshore submarine threat had been neutralised.

While this success story in Vestfiord was being enacted in the north the 'Teamwork' scenario had been grinding inexorably on. The Orange threat had steadily increased. Submarines were 'observed redeploying to northern locations' and aircraft were massing at northern bases. Surface forces were also beginning to trail Blue vessels or waiting in close proximity to the Norwegian coast.

Early on 11 September, covered by the carrier and ASW Striking Forces, the amphibious force rendezvoused for a demonstration and rehearsal landing in the vicinity of Hemnesfiord in the Trondelag area. To the northwest just above 65° was the ASW Striking Force, with the carrier battle groups to the southwest. The landing area had been cleared of mines by a Belgian-Dutch-German MCM force, composed of five minehunters and five minesweepers led by the support tender *Werra* of the Federal German Navy and supported by the seagoing tug *Nordeney*.

In addition to the US amphibious task group that had crossed the Atlantic, the UK-Netherlands amphibious force had left Plymouth on the 5th and had been covered by British MCM vessels through the Irish Sea. It had played no part in the Freeplay, although three of its escorts, *Bristol, Scylla* and *Tourville,* had gone on ahead and been in combat as Grey forces supporting the Canadians. Other escorts were the Type 42 destroyer *York,* providing extra air defence, and the Type 21 frigate *Avenger.* RFAs *Bayleaf* and *Regent* carried fuel and supplies. The amphibious ships themselves were led by the LPD HMS *Intrepid,* task group flagship, the RFA-operated Landing Ships Logistic *Sir Galahad, Sir Tristram, Sir Bedivere, Sir Geraint* and *Sir Percivale,* and the British Army landing ship *Ardennes.* In

addition six ships were taken up from trade (STUFT); the modern ferries *Bolero* and *Dana Regina,* the roll-on/roll-off (ro-ro) ships, *Norrona, Mercandia Gigant* and *Tor Caledonia,* and the semi-submersible heavy lift vessel *Este Submerger.*

This armada, with its embarked troops (see Chapter 6), sailed under Northwood's command but on the 11th it rendezvoused with the Striking Fleet and came under its operational control. The rest of the Task Force was composed of the US amphibious ships and the replenishment ship USS *Savannah.*

The Trondelag rehearsal was intended to allow the various forces to coalesce into a single group and snags to appear before actual operations began. Once more the dangers of operating in Norwegian inshore waters became apparent. At 23.48 on the 11th the British LSL *Sir Geraint* went aground at the mouth of Hemnesfiord, suffering propeller damage. Two of the minehunters tried to remove her during the night but failed and a civilian tug had to be called for. All personnel and equipment was cross-decked and the accident had no effect on the landing which went in on time using landing craft and helicopters. Flying conditions were not good, with low cloud ceiling which curtailed operations with the US Marines' AV-8B Harriers. Air support from the carriers was also prevented by the weather, although *Forrestal's* initial A-7 air strike arrived punctually. By the evening all of the amphibious units were underway after re-embarking their troops, but once more misfortune struck at night. This time it was the American tank landing ship *Boulder* that went aground, at 02.00 on the morning of the 13th. Refloating her proved difficult and she was out of the exercise.

In the scenario the rehearsal and the following day's supporting arms exercise (SACEX) were useful demonstrations of resolve. In the real world they might well have done the trick to de-escalate the situation. However, that would have defeated much of the training aim of 'Teamwork 88'. So the carriers, followed by the amphibious ships, moved north. Leading them all as usual was the ASW Striking Force, both covering and supported by the *Roosevelt* group. The aim was to insert the latter battle group into Vestfiord on the 14th while the *Forrestal* group would follow, moving further north into Andfiord the following day. This would also cover the movement of the amphibious ships towards their planned landing areas around Tovik and Gratangen.

Orange was becoming ever more threatening. Blue had been advised to quit the Norwegian Sea and Orange amphibious forces were on the move. Orange surface combatants, notably the 'Slava' and the modified 'Kashin' were moving towards the amphibians. The two sides were engaging in mutual jamming and electronic harassment.

Adm White and his staff in the ASW Striking Fleet had their usual vital role to play. They kept their well practised eyes on the submarine threat. The US towed array destroyers *Spruance* and *Moosbrugger* were playing leading roles, as was the USS *Leyte Gulf,* the Aegis cruiser escorting the *Roosevelt*

that was also a useful asset ahead of the carrier with her towed array long range sonar. Compiling an ASW picture was, however, even more difficult than usual as the enemy SSNs were running very quietly and slowly. Preventing some kind of pre-emptive attack was, therefore, unlikely. The three Orange coastal boats were placed two in Vestfiord and one

Below:
HMS *Penelope*, Britain's contribution to SNFL, was seriously gashed along her side when a replenishment at sea manoeuvre went disastrously wrong on the morning of 11 September.
H. M. Steele

Right:
The tricky waters of Vestfiord claimed more victims on 13 September. First the Belgian frigate *Westhinder* went aground, then, in coming to the rescue, the Canadian destroyer *Athabaskan* hit the rock as well, damaging her sonar and plating. The Canadian Task Group Commander could console himself, however, that the Vestfiord precursor operations had gone better than ever before.
Naval Forces

Below right:
Much in demand were the repair facilities of the depot ship USS *Puget Sound*, forward deployed into northern Norway as an experiment that proved to have been far-sighted. *Puget Sound's* role in the exercise was proof of the enormous operational utility of such afloat support, especially in forward operations.

in the approaches to Andfiord, with the larger conventional submarines either in waiting or positioning themselves in the Vestfiord approaches; one had been picked up snorting. White's advice to the Striking Fleet was to keep close to the coast forcing the torpedo-armed 'Victors' to operate in unsuitable shallow water and the 'Charlies' to fire against targets masked to their missiles by the terrain. The best defence against coastal submarines was high-speed, evasive routeing, darkening ship, active sonar operations by escort groups offset from the MEUs, rader flooding of large areas and emission controls, especially of distinctive transmitters. Both before and during the carrier break-in, White planned to deploy his forces relatively statically, both inside and outside Vestfiord in order to put maximum pressure on the most likely threat axes with the intention of inflicting the maximum fatigue and frustration upon the enemy submarine commanders,

Top:
Truly formidable threats to any invaders of Norway and highly elusive targets for NATO forces exercising precursor operations in the fiords are the little Norwegian Type 207 coast defence submarines. This is *Kaura* used in 'Teamwork' along with her sisters *Ulstein* and *Kinn*. *USNI*

Above:
Norwegian FPBs were also used to attack 'Blue' forces, two were *Snögg* class seen here with their four torpedo tubes and up to four Penguin missiles. This is *Kvikk*; the boats used in 'Teamwork' were *Rask* (P983) and *Kjapp* (P985). *USNI*

so forcing them into making mistakes before the *Theodore Roosevelt* moved in. During the break-in the aim was to create confusion and irrecoverable error.

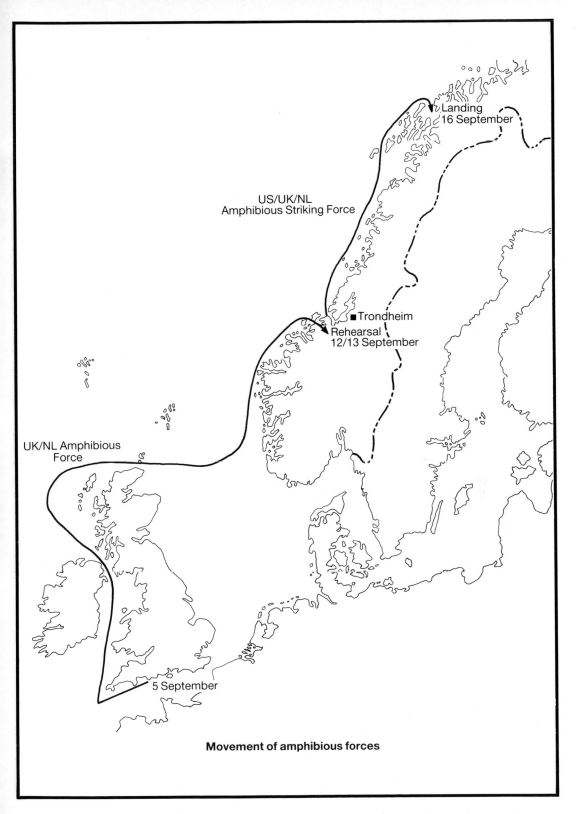

Landing
16 September

US/UK/NL
Amphibious Striking Force

■ Trondheim

Rehearsal
12/13 September

UK/NL Amphibious
Force

5 September

Movement of amphibious forces

Top:
The other FPBs were of the later 'Hauk' class with two torpedo tubes and six missiles. This is *Erle* last built. The boats used were *Hauk* herself (P986) and *Falk* (P995).

Above:
Providing area air defence protection for the UK-NL amphibious force was the British Type 42 destroyer HMS *York*. *Royal Navy*

Left:
Anti-submarine and anti-surface protection, plus some AA capability (she shot down one jet aircraft in the Falklands War with her 4.5in gun) was provided to the amphibious forces by the Type 21 frigate HMS *Avenger*. *Royal Navy*

White further recommended that the carriers move up their most capable ASW escorts and put them in the lead but offset to the west. In order to minimise the enemy's capacity to recover from making errors and reposition, it was also recommended that the various task groups keep as close as possible to

each other. This also provided for better mutual protection. White wanted the fleet to delay its departure for as long as possible in order to give his advanced ASW forces time to put pressure on the enemy and to minimise the latter's detection and reaction time. COMASWSTRIKFOR would reposition his forces with their supporting MPA when the time came to cover the Andfiord advance.

It was agreed, therefore, that a decoy group should lead the way in the afternoon of 13 September to trail its coat out to sea, with the *Theodore Roosevelt* escorted by the CGN *South Carolina* and the Dutch Task Group following in the early evening

Orange air forces

Base	Nationality	Aircraft	Exercise Identity (Role)	Dates (from end of Freeplay)
Lossiemouth	FGR	8 Tornado	'Fencer' (attack)	10-18 Sept
	UK	Buccaneers	'Fencer'/'Badger' (SS-N-9) (attack/surface-to-surface missile)	10-21 Sept
Machrihanish	US	1 EC-24	'Badger J' (ECM)	10-12 Sept
	US	1 EP-3A	'Badger J'/'Bear D' (ECM/Recce)	10-12 Sept
	US	2 ERA-3B	'Badger J' (ECM)	10-13 Sept
	US	4 EA-6A	'Badger J' (ECM)	10-13 Sept
Bodø	Norway (also doubled as Blue)	24 F-16	'Fencer' (attack)	10-21 Sept
Bardufoss	US (ANG)	6 F-4	'Fencer' (attack)	16-21 Sept
	US	1 NKC-135	'Badger J' (ECM)	12-19 Sept
	US	1 EC-24	'Badger J' (ECM)	12-19 Sept
	US	1 EP-3A	'Badger J'/'Bear D' (ECM/Recce)	13-19 Sept
	UK	Falcon	'Badger G'/'Badger J' (attack/ECM)	12-21 Sept
	Norway	Falcon	'Badger J' (ECM)	13-21 Sept
Andoya	UK	9 Buccaneer	'Fencer'/'Badger G'/SS-N-9 (attack/attack/surface-to-surface misssile)	12-21 Sept
Banak	Norway	14 F-16	'Fencer' (attack)	12-21 Sept
Flesland	UK	8 Canberra	'Badger J'/AS-5 (attack/anti-radiation missile)	12-21 Sept

on their coast-hugging route to come into Vestfiord by 05.00 the following morning, the 14th. *Leyte Gulf* would act as air warfare co-ordinator. The *Forrestal* group would leave in the middle of the night to cover the movement of the amphibious ships that would depart about the same time. Before the sun went down on the 13th, an uncharacteristically fine evening, the decoy group had indeed appeared off the mouth of Vestfiord. The stage was set for the 'Battle of the Fiords' to begin in earnest.

Left:
Also deployed was the new replacement for the old *Sir Galahad*, lost in the Falklands War. The new ship is significantly larger than the older vessels. *Swan Hunter*

Top:
In addition to specialist amphibious shipping, merchant ships taken up from trade (STUFT) were also used to transport the UK-NL force, among them, the Fred Olsen ro-ro ferry *Bolero* seen on the left is being refuelled by RFA *Bayleaf*; *Intrepid* is on the right. *Royal Navy*

Above:
Another accident on the unlucky 13 September affected the LST USS *Boulder* that suffered quite serious damage when she ran aground after re-embarking troops after the rehearsal landing. This shows her on 'Teamwork 80'. *USNI*

Right:
A casualty of the Trondelag rehearsal landing was the British LSL *Sir Geraint* that ran aground at the mouth of Hemnesfiord. *Royal Navy*

Top left:
An A-7 Corsair prepares to take-off from *Forrestal* with a Walleye guided weapon under the starboard wing. This was during the rehearsal landing.

Centre left:
As Carrier Striking Group 2 operated off the Trondelag landings it was screened by the Aegis cruiser *Mobile Bay* and the German task group, one of whose frigates can be seen in the background. *USNI*

Bottom left:
Two of the West German frigates providing close ASW protection for *Forrestal* on 12 September were *Bremen* (left) and *Emden* (right). *USNI*

Top right:
The German destroyer *Lutjens* had become part of *Forrestal's* escort after playing 'enemy' in the earlier part of the exercise. *USNI*

Bottom right:
Forrestal's Tomcat fighters are the key to her ability to fight and win the outer air battle around the carrier battle group. They were photographed while she was supporting the Trondelag rehearsal landing. *USNI*

5 War in the Fiords

On the 14th, as tension between Blue and Orange moved inexorably towards war, the *Theodore Roosevelt* battle group established itself in Vestfiord. The carrier patrolled slowly up and down the northwestern side of the fiord to the northeast of the island of Vaeroy, relatively close to the Lofotens, although not as close as she would have been in war. The availability of sufficient wind over the deck also meant that the carrier did not have to sustain high speeds for flight operations. The Dutch frigate *Bloys Van Treslong* had little trouble acting as plane guard and the USS *South Carolina* hardly needed her nuclear propulsion to stay with her massive charge. In order to deal with the submarine threat the carrier area was being systematically searched within three boxes by the rest of the Dutch Task Group, the *De Ruyter* in the centre, the *Van Almonde* to the southwest and the *Piet Heyn* to the northeast. The irrepressible Nowegian FPBs attacked the *Piet Heyn* that evening, despite the fact that Orange and Blue were still not officially at war. The completed Canadian Task Group looked after the entrance to Vestfiord from the ASW angle with HMCS *Annapolis*, returned from the ASW Striking Fleet, acting as a towed array gate guard. *Annapolis* rotated with *Fraser* which had a defective helicopter but both ships were back with the Striking Fleet for 'deep field' operations by the 16th, *Fraser* with a replacement Sea King. By then *Athabaskan's* damaged plates had forced her to join *Westhinder* in Bodø, leaving the Canadian Task Group with but a single Canadian vessel, *Saguenay*, acting as group commander. The Norwegian Task Group's frigates *Oslo* and *Bergen* that had helped escort the amphibious force north and which were tasked in this phase with supporting the CVBGs provided the rest of the 'Canadian' group before they left to escort the coastal convoy (see Chapter 7).

Dipping sonar helicopters covered the area of Vestfiord to the southeast of the carrier operating box and further southeast still the formidable Aegis cruiser *Leyte Gulf* patrolled a long beat up and down, keeping a watchful eye for aircraft and a clear field of

Below:
The new classic form of carrier operation, in the protected bastions of the wide northern Norwegian fiords. *USNI*

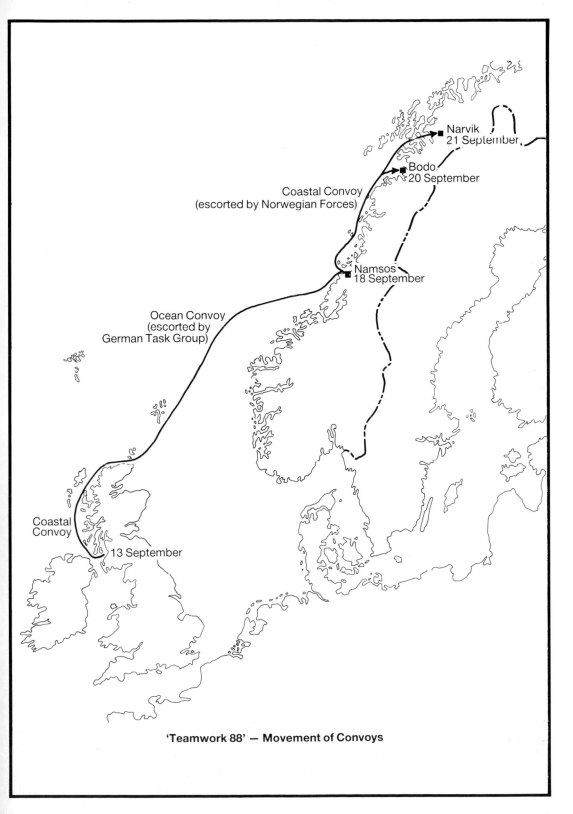

Narvik
21 September

Bodo
20 September

Coastal Convoy
(escorted by Norwegian Forces)

Namsos
18 September

Ocean Convoy
(escorted by
German Task Group)

Coastal
Convoy

13 September

'Teamwork 88' — Movement of Convoys

Above left:
The giant bulk of the USS *Theodore Roosevelt* as she slowly moves through the waters of Vestfiord on 'Teamwork 88'. The *Roosevelt* group was safely established in the fiord by 14 September.
Royal Dutch Navy

Left:
The *Roosevelt's* faithful close-in defender, from both air and submarine threats, was the nuclear powered cruiser *South Carolina*. Capable of identical performance to the carrier she could follow her wherever she went, sometimes out of the fiord on sudden 'combat surges'. Once the *Roosevelt* group was in the fiord the commander of the Destroyer Squadron 24, embarked on *South Carolina*, was ASW commander for the fiord operation. *USNI*

Above:
Patrolling her beat in the middle of the fiord was the 'Aegis' cruiser *Leyte Gulf*, covering both longer range air and subsurface threats with her radar and towed array sonar. *USNI*

fire for her radar and missiles. She also had her SQR-19 towed array sonar out and her SQS-53 hull sonar on active/passive ASW search. The two decoy destroyers also stayed on this side of the fiord,

drawing attention away from the carrier and engaging in ASW patrols (*Pratt*) and escort duties for the logistical vessel (*Charles F. Adams*). S-3s from the *Theodore Roosevelt* carried out radar flooding everywhere to keep the enemy submarines' heads down; they also dropped sono buoys. There were two submarine kills on this day. An SH-3 helicopter conducting a random search got a dipping sonar contact and attacked. Both a second dipper and the *Van Treslong* obtained uncertain contacts on this submarine and then two SH-3s carried out a successful attack. Later the *Almonde's* Lynx sighted a snorting submarine. It immediately attacked then dipped its sonar to regain contact. It continued to prosecute the contact and an S-3 was called in, which also gained contact and successfully attacked. This was the first time in carrier operation in Vestfiord that the carrier battle groups had got in the first successful shots against 'hostile' submarines, rather than vice versa.

The amphibians arrived overnight on the 14th/15th. Those watching radar screens in Vestfiord just before midnight were surprised to see about a dozen contacts suddenly appear on their radar out of the leads to the south. At about 10-12kt they tramped their way straight across the fiord and just at the

Left:
While cruising up and down Vestfiord, USS *Theodore Roosevelt* kept up a high tempo of flight operations. Here an F/A-18 is launched on a CAP mission. *Royal Dutch Navy*

Bottom left:
An A-6 all-weather strike aircraft and an F/A-18 fighter/clear weather strike aircraft demonstrate the carrier's offensive potential while an F-14 all-weather interceptor is catapulted off the flightdeck and an F-18 prepares for the same. The mountains of the Lofoten Islands loom out of the mist in the distance. *Royal Dutch Navy*

Top right:
The combination of the E-2 Hawkeye and F-14 Tomcat gives the *Theodore Roosevelt* in Vestfiord the power to take on virtually any airborne adversary with a good chance of success. Drawing the Soviet Naval Air Force into an attack on the carriers favourably placed in their fiord bastions is a key feature of the Forward Maritime Strategy.
Royal Dutch Navy

Centre right:
Backing up the *South Carolina* in keeping the *Roosevelt's* operational area clear of submarines for the first part of the carrier's time in Vestfiord was the Dutch Navy's task group, one of whose ships was the frigate *Bloys Van Treslong*. She acted as 'plane guard' for the carrier while *De Ruyter* and two other 'Kortenners' patrolled three 'boxes' in which the big ship moved. *Ian Allan Library*

Bottom right:
Operating in the 'deep field' outside Vestfiord were the ships of the ASW Striking Force, among them *Fraser* seen here just after the exercise in October 1988. *Fraser* was also used under Canadian Task Group command to act as a gate guard for Vestfiord. Her helicopter gave some problems and she rotated aircraft with the frigate *Annapolis*.

point it seemed they must pile up turned hard to port and formed themselves into line ahead to move through Rosthavet at a careful 8kt. By 01.30 the gaggle of amphibious ships and their Anglo-French escorts (*York, Bristol, Avenger, Scylla* and *Tourville*) were clear of the strait and moving Northeast. What they did next will be covered in the next chapter.

The following day, which dawned very foggy indeed, saw war finally break out between Orange and Blue. The actual time that general alert was received was 13.04GMT and at 14.20 an air raid developed on the force in Vestfiord. During it, the forces there went to weapons free and *Leyte Gulf* fired at least six simulated missiles against the Orange aircraft. As more air raids came in in succeeding hours all the CVBG escorts were engaging threats with simulated missiles, trying to sort out which targets had already been engaged by defending fighters. The weather interfered with flight

operations from the *Roosevelt* and late that afternoon *Leyte Gulf* had a fire fight with the exercise 'Osa' class missile attack craft which appeared out of the murk. One was 'sunk' by 5in shellfire. One of the Vestfiord submarines also got in a shot at the carrier battle group, as a telltale green flare showed.

The carrier had rather asked for it, sailing at 5kt for over an hour in the direction of an area where there had been multiple confirmed contacts with the Orange submarines. There had been three attacks on these boats and one had been adjudged successful so in the real world the carrier might have

been safe. An SH-3 counterattacked the source of the green flare after the 'ghost' of the killed submarine had obtained the hit on the carrier and killed the obstinate orange submarine yet again.

The deep water ASW battle was still, of course, being fought. On the first evening of the Orange-Blue war Rear-Adm White reviewed the situation and the role of his force. His aim was an intensive search effort in the approaches to Vestfiord and Andfiord to detect, locate and prosecute Orange submarines to destruction. Both radar and active sonar as well as passive means were to be utilised as aggressively as

Above:
To experiment with conducting ASWSTRIKFOR operations from a safer haven, Rear-Adm White brought HMS *Illustrious* into the sheltered waters for Hadselfiord. From here he could cover both CVBG operational areas in Vestfiord and Andfiord.

possible. He laid out his units in a search pattern, regaining towed array assets from the fiord forces to boost his Striking Force. In addition to *Illustrious* he had the submarine USS *Baltimore*, HMCS *Annapolis*, soon to be joined by her 'alter ego' *Fraser*, USS *Spruance*, USS *Moosbrugger* and HMS *Brave*. HMS *Cleopatra*, with her ultra-sensitive 2031 towed array, was operating as a pair with the American frigate *Elmer Montgomery* as an active/passive combination. *Evertsen* was due to rejoin this 'combo' on the evening of the following day. The decoy destroyers were to transit from Vestfiord up to Andfiord and back to try to promote submarine movement and to provide detection and killing opportunities. Two maritime patrol aircraft would be on continuous patrol working with the ASW Striking Force, while carrier-based S-3s would be utilised as opportunity offered. *Illustrious* planned an intensive flying schedule both for its ASW Sea Kings and the AEW helicopters, so useful for radar flooding as well as filling in the air and surface picture. If enemy surface action groups re-emerged as a threat (after their rapid demolition once war had begun) ISAR surveillance and air strikes would deal with them. *Illustrious* was to use her Sea Harriers to integrate with the overall defensive air battle over the sea. White put his logistical units, *Olmeda* and *Gold Rover*, into fiord LOGHAVENS; the flagship *Illustrious* was strategically placed in an operating bastion in Hadselfiord.

The great advantage of the fiord strategy is that available assets can be concentrated where they can do most good. Providing 'deep field' ASW protection for the carriers from a 360° threat axis would have been even more difficult than the task Adm White was presented with here. As it was he was taking on the enemy on the least unfavourable terms possible.

On the 16th both sides had the benefit of better weather in Vestfiord. As the *Theodore Roosevelt* launched a stream of CAP and attack sorties, Orange Buccaneers, long since 'shot down' by F-14s, screamed impressively across the calm water. The *Treslong* kept up her faithful plane guard, while *South Carolina* provided a last-ditch missile screen four miles up threat from the huge carrier manoeuvring into wind at only about 8kt. This was not too realistic as moving slowly in deep water was the worst possible conduct in a submarine threat area; the correct choices were slow movement in the shallows up against the 'wall' of the Lofotens or very high speed in the deep water in the centre. Still, the constant pressure from airborne radars, dipping sonars and ship-mounted active sonars kept the submarines at bay. The carrier had also begun to learn and it obeyed the screen commander's advice to remain clear of known submarine operating areas. There were no tell-tale green flares indicating a claimed submarine attack between midnight and

12.00. As Capt J. M. Miller, the ASW commander in the *South Carolina*, put it to his force at midday: 'The bottom line is that ASW in Vestfiord is frustrating and it requires patience by all concerned, but one green flare in three days with several high confidence sub kills is better than previous experience. Keep the pressure on — classify with ordnance.'

Late that afternoon there was a flare-up of ASW activity with two green flares against *Almonde*. Two helicopters carried out six attacks: the submarine was assessed sunk. Towards the fiord mouth *Bergen* and *Saguenay* attacked some dubious contacts.

That night *Theodore Roosevelt*, *South Carolina* and *Leyte Gulf* conducted a 'combat surge' to dump rubbish in deep water, an exercise artificiality but a reality necessary to protect the environment. One had been planned the previous night but had been cancelled due to heavy weather. The seas were still quite rough as three of the world's most impressive warships knifed through the high waves and spray. The activity was not without risk, however, as the ships took a direct course out of the fiord and returned on a reciprocal bearing. This was against the best ASW advice and was asking for trouble again, which came in the shape of green flares.

The carriers continued their operations on succeeding days until fiord operations ceased on 21 September. They quicky disposed of the Orange surface threat in 'War at Sea' air strikes, and integrated their powerful F-14 and F/A-18 air defence fighter components into the overall shore-based air defence system, with its USAF F-15s, US Marine Corps F/A-18s and Royal Norwegian Air Force F-16s. Air strikes were also flown with the carrier aircraft being escorted by USAF and Royal Norwegian Air Force fighter escorts as well as USN fighters to targets at Selemaen. The accent was on integration, with all air assets working as a co-ordinated whole, and the exercise developed co-ordination and air control procedures so that the air picture for northern Norway could be refined as much as possible. NATO E-3s worked side by side with the carriers' E-2s, as did the Striking Fleet air organisation and NADGE (NATO Air Defence Ground Environment), the Alliance's shore-based air defence system. This kind of real-world exercising is essential given the inherent and traditional difficulties of interfacing different nationalities, command organisations and armed services into a coherent whole. The pay-offs are enormous, the Striking Fleet has an enormous synergistic impact on the air situation in the north, and the shore-based aircraft have a similar impact on the safety of the Striking Fleet.

For 'Teamwork', Blue was deploying 14 Royal Norwegian Air Force F-16 fighters at Bodø. This airfield was also being used as a forward US Marine Corps air base with 12 F/A-18s, four EA-6Bs backed up by three KC-130s and a C-12. At Evenes near Narvik the Marines had 12 AV-8B Harriers on the forward operating base at the airport, together with a couple of OV-2s. Bardufoss and Banak were Orange bases but three USAF F-15s on detachment at the former were partly available to the 'good guys', and Bardufoss was also used as a pre-landing operating base for the 18 helicopters of the UKNL amphibious force. Four NATO early warning E-3s were at Öerland, together with Blue MPA, three USN P-3Cs and three Dutch P-3Cs. Other MPA assets were three RAF Nimrods and five Norwegian P-3Bs at Andoya and three Bundesmarine Atlantiques at Sola. Five US KC-135 tankers at the latter base supported both sides. All these aircraft totalled only 85 (not counting the OV-10s and helicopters), about the complement of a single US carrier.

In the real world all the Orange aircraft would have been available too, notably Banak's 14 Norwegian F-16s, but so would a third (and possibly even a fourth) carrier to the Striking Fleet. The shore and sea-based elements of the Norwegian Sea battle are, therefore, two sides of the same coin, even more so with the carriers in the fiords, with the added dimensions of mobility, both defensive and offensive, that the great ships provide.

Possibly in order to simulate a third carrier, *Forrestal* joined *Roosevelt* in Vestfiord later in the exercise. This was the first time two carriers had operated together in the fiord environment and it

gave useful experience in the concept. Moving carriers and their escorts around gave the submarines their chances too, and over the entire week of fiord operations from 14-21 September no less than 23 green flares were released. Of these flaming data some 10 were counterattacked to confirmed kills. In all some 34 ASW attacks were conducted in the fiord phase of which half were on real contacts. This was over three times the success rate of previous Vestfiord exercises, an index of the improvement in fiord ASW expertise that only such exercises can provide.

It must be remembered that fiord operations are only one tactic in the execution of NATO's Forward Maritime Strategy but they are a crucial one. They allow the most to be made of available forces, a constructive and creative use of synergy and geography to defend both Norway and the Alliance as a whole as far forward as practical. This also requires operations ashore, however, and it is to these and their strategic background that we will now turn.

Below:
One major advantage of fiord operations is the close integration of carrier battle group operations with land-based air power, typified by this Royal Norwegian Air Force F-16 fighter. During 'Teamwork', 14 of these were flying from Bodø for 'Blue'. *Ian Allan Library*

6 Teamwork: Amphibious Landings and Operations Ashore

By Graham Thompson

Norway is a small nation in a strategically exposed position. Although Norway's security policy forbids the permanent basing of foreign troops on its soil in peacetime, it would need quick and effective support in war. As Johan Jorgen Holst, the Norwegian Defence Minister has said, 'the absence of foreign troops on Norwegian soil in peacetime creates a need to reinforce Norway earlier and more rapidly than might otherwise be the case. Preparations have to be made for the reception of Allied reinforcements, and exercises have to be performed regularly in order to make credible the plans for reinforcement.'

The strategic geography of NATO's northern region is of crucial importance. A distance of 1,750 miles separates Kirkenes in north Norway and the Baltic. If Norway were swung southwards on an axis superimposed on Oslo, Tromso would lie on Naples. Yet on land the region lacks depth – near Narvik, Norway is only four miles wide.

Climatically, northern Norway can be a cold, wet, desolate place. However, summer temperatures often reach 30°C with sunshine 24hr a day. The problems militarily are the rapid and unpredictable changes which can occur in the climatic conditions. The terrain in the barren region north of the Arctic Circle is demanding, with roads limited and railways non-existent. The special terrain and climate of the region pose innumerable problems for both defending and attacking forces.

Transport links to the north are limited. The Norwegian rail system stops at Bodø, and the main road route is the E6 highway, which is not built to handle large amounts of heavy military equipment. The military and civil airfields are combined and are at Bodø, Tromso, Evenes, Bardufoss, Andoya, Alta, Barak and Kirkenes.

The area is much more famous for its winters, which last from October until May. Going for wheeled vehicles is impossible off the roads for much of the winter and even on the roads it is only possible if they are continually cleared. Tracked vehicles with low ground pressure can operate almost everywhere for most of the year but can be bogged down easily during thaw conditions during April/May and onwards. Helicopters are therefore of the utmost importance in all kinds of operations. In certain parts of the country the only way to move troops or supply troops is by sea.

Latitude, too poses difficulties. Almost all of Norway's three northern counties are north of the Arctic Circle. One of the most notable differences for those from more southerly latitudes is the effect of light. Natural light has a much stronger quality. Moonlight, starlight and snow-reflected light have a far greater significance at this latitude. The Aurora Borealis is often visible in north Norway.

For much of Finnmark and Troms the sun does not go below the horizon for between 8-10 weeks during the summer. However, the transition to shortening winter days is very fast, and for an equal period it remains dark or near-dark in the winter. This means that, for example, street-lighting remains on during the day and the continual darkness has a depressing effect on the people. The Norwegian authorities are finding it difficult to make people stay in the north and have even introduced special tax incentives to encourage Norwegians to remain.

The Norwegian coastal areas are elaborate archipelagos containing fiords and partly-submerged mountains which can rise up to 3,000m from the sea. The vegetation of the area varies from

grassy flat-lands at the coast, scrub-vegetation on the plateaux with some sparse forestation, to great pine forests.

The practical effects of the environment on military operations in Norway are summarised in the standard US Army manual, FM 31-71, entitled 'Northern Operations'. The manual states:

'The northern environment is a dynamic force. He who recognises and understands this force can use it; he who disregards or underestimates this force is threatened with failure or destruction. Because of the demanding requirements on the individual soldier, leadership must be of the highest calibre . . . in the north the human element is all-important. The effectiveness of equipment is greatly reduced. Specialized training and experience are essential. *The climate does not allow a margin of error for the individual or the organisation.'*

On the specific implications for military operations, the manual goes on:

'The ground mobility of all units is restricted. Movements must be carefully planned and executed with the knowledge that distance can be as difficult to overcome as the enemy. Momentum is difficult to achieve and quickly lost.

'Tactical principles for operations in the north are the same as those employed in other areas. However, because of the environment, emphasis may be placed on principles which are less important in areas of milder climate.'

Areas of different emphasis include:
● in winter operations, during the long periods of darkness, night movement and night combat become the rule rather than the exception. Columns moving in daylight are easy to locate and destroy
● lines of communications are the lifeblood of operations in the north. Forces may be defeated by severing their air and sea communications, since the terrain and climate may deny the use of alternatives
● deception is vital because of the special vulnerability of forces deployed in the north
● in winter, denial of adequate shelter can cause casualties as surely as the delivery of firepower
● more time has to be allowed for the movement of units and supplies
● magnetic and ionospheric storms can play havoc with radio communications.

All in all, northern Norway is a challenging environment. Troops who are used to it can cope – but those who are not, of whatever nationality, will suffer grievously.

The Soviet Union has been giving increased attention to the northern area. It has built up a large military infrastructure on the Kola Peninsula, near the Norwegian border in the far north. The former US Secretary of the Navy, John Lehman, once called Kola 'the most valuable piece of real estate in the world'. Its Northern Fleet now accounts for almost

Above:
Royal Marines with the SA-80, the new 5.56mm rifle now in service in the British forces. *Crown Copyright*

Above right:
Royal Marines in an open-topped landing craft — very unpleasant in the Norwegian weather. In the distance is the Landing Ships Logistic *Sir Geraint*. *Crown Copyright*

60% of the Soviet Navy's submarines, 25% of the surface warships and 25% of its aircraft.

There are two main concentrations of Soviet land forces facing Norway in peacetime, based in the Leningrad Military District.

Around Murmansk, the standing forces include: a motor-rifle division; an independent artillery brigade; two air assault brigades; one missile brigade. On mobilisation, an extra motor-rifle division may be available in the Murmansk area.

Around Kandalaksa, there is: one motor-rifle division; an independent SAM brigade. Both groups of forces come under the command of the army, based at Petrozavodsk.

Both motor-rifle divisions have been specially equipped for northern operations. They have an increased complement of the more mobile and lighter MT-LB armoured fighting vehicles (instead of the more usual BMP-1), and slightly fewer than usual main battle tanks, thought to be T-72s. In addition, their artillery regiments have self-propelled guns. However, none of this would permit major off-road operations in northern Norway.

Of some interest is the Soviet naval infantry (Marines) unit based at Pechenga, the 'Kirkenes'

Below:
Royal Marines of 45 Commando landing at Groufiord on D-Day of Exercise 'Teamwork'. *SACLANT*

Above:
The landings in the Astafiord: USS *Nassau* is in the background, an LAV-25 on the left. *SACLANT*

Brigade. This brigade has recently been expanded from regimental size and extensively re-equipped. The unit is probably Category A, and could be put into action with little warning. It is also believed that a motor-rifle division is specially trained for sea transport. This does not mean it could carry out an amphibious assault on a defended beach, rather it could reinforce a harbour already secured by the naval infantry.

The Soviet amphibious assets in the Northern Fleet are considerable. They include: two 'Alligator' class, capable of carrying 300 men, and 25-30 armoured vehicles; four 'Ropucha' class, capable of carrying 230 troops and 25 armoured vehicles; five 'Polnocny' class, capable of carrying 110 troops and 6-8 armoured vehicles. There are also believed to be some hovercraft.

If the Warsaw Pact undertook an amphibious assault in northern Norway, it would have five phases:
1. Preparation of equipment and units
2. Loading of personnel and equipment on to ships
3. Moving by sea to objective area and debarkation
4. Battle for the beachhead by the amphibious units
5. Landing of gound forces and withdrawal of naval infantry.

The battle for the beachhead begins with naval gunfire on coastal targets. An airborne or heliborne assault inland to block the movement of enemy reserves may also take place, although the terrain may make this difficult or impossible. Minesweepers would then clear the approach routes. Once this is done, the first wave, probably of PT-76 amphibious tanks, would disembark. They may engage enemy targets as they swim ashore. The following wave is

made up of BTR-60 armoured personnel carriers. Troops do not dismount from their vehicles on the beach unless they meet determined resistance. They will try to press inland to seize the objectives or meet up with ground forces, as appropriate.

Several weaknesses have been identified by Western intelligence as applying to Warsaw Pact amphibious forces. These include:

● Loss of surprise – the amphibious force would be vulnerable to attack if detected moving towards the assault area
● Air cover – SA-7 and SA-9 missiles can be fired from the decks of the landing ships or from the shore. There is some doubt as to whether this would be sufficient
● Sea conditions – a severe sea state, as is often the rule in Norwegian waters, could seriously disrupt an assault
● Obstacles – a well-prepared system of obstacles and mines could slow or stop an assault
● Enemy armour – this would pose a serious threat to the lightly-armoured assault force. Anti-tank guided weapons, such as the British Milan or US Tow, could do the same
● Rates of advance – if the first wave is prevented from leaving the beachhead by NATO action or by restricting terrain, massing could occur and the momentum could be lost
● Beach conditions – an assault without sufficient reconnaissance could prove disastrous.

All this means that, whether they come overland or by sea, a Warsaw Pact invasion of northern Norway would be a very difficult military operation. If the country could be reinforced by other NATO nations, the Soviet task probably becomes impossible.

The Norwegian Army in peacetime is only 19,000 strong, but this can be expanded in war by 146,000

reservists in less than 72hr. In addition, there are some 85,000 Home Guard who are available for rear-area defence. In all, on mobilisation Norway puts 8.1% of its population into uniform, which compares very favourable with 1.5% for the USA or 1.1% for the UK.

On mobilisation, the Army forms three armoured brigades; four mechanised brigades and six light infantry brigades. Substantial forces would be transferred from southern Norway to reinforce the

Left:
US Marines of 2 Battalion, 8th Marines move inland from the beachhead. *SACLANT*

Centre left:
The Norwegian terrain is very demanding. At the right of the picture, the E6 highway, the main route north, with a 3,000ft mountain beyond. The 'Hummer' vehicles belong to the USMC Regimental Landing Team, whose command post was established here, just north of Bjerkvik. The helicopter landing on the morning of 16 September by 1/25 Infantry USMC took place to the east of the E6, off to the right of this photograph.
G. N. Thompson

Bottom left:
An LVTP-7 armoured vehicle of 2/8th Infantry USMC comes ashore at Tovik, around 07.15 on 16 September. *G. N. Thompson*

Bottom:
In staggered file, the Royals move inland from Tovik, the 'tail-end charlie' guarding their rear.
G. N. Thompson

Bottom right:
An 'enemy' NM-116 light tank of the Norwegian Army guards the road to Flodvik. Shortly after this photograph was taken, this tank and two others were engaged in a fierce 'firefight' with Milan anti-tank crews of Support Company, 45 Commando. The TV crew had made good their escape by then. *G. N. Thompson*

northern area. In peacetime, the only standing force in northern Norway is 'Brigade North', based at Troms, with some tanks and artillery. It was this unit which provided the 'enemy' on 'Teamwork 88'.

It is worth dwelling on the need for an effective Norwegian mobilisation system and how it works. Of all the European NATO countries, Norway has one of the largest land areas but the smallest population. In addition, the bulk of the population live in the south of the country – only about 10% live in the north, the area which is of greatest military significance. Norway gets round this paradox by the 'Total Defence Concept'. The concept aims, in time of war, 'to achieve the largest possible military forces with the highest possible quality and, simultaneously, to obtain maximum support for the civilian infrastructure and resources'.

As Gen Frederick Bull-Hansen, the Norwegian Chief of Defence Staff, put it:

'A total defence arrangement rests on the fact that a modern industrialised society in peacetime possesses vast resources and a surplus of goods suited for military use in war . . . for example, we could comfortably transport half the population by truck in one operation . . . we activate transport firms, workshops and stores: we mobilise oil companies who deliver right up to the front. Some large civilian helicopter companies operating offshore in peacetime can be mobilised and organised into squadrons with their 80-100 helicopters; in investment alone this saves us around £400m.'

Norway operates a conscription system, to provide both peacetime standing forces and a large reserve in war. Its wartime organisations are mostly light infantry brigades, equipped and highly-trained for fighting in the country's demanding climate and terrain.

The Home Guard is organised in small units, whose members keep their weapons and ammunition at home. Thus, it is possible to provide, locally

and within a matter of hours, a force which can secure the key installations and communications routes on which the rest of the armed forces rely.

The Norwegian Army armoured force consists of 80 Leopard I main battle tanks, 42 M-48A5 tanks, and 70 NM-116 light tanks. Old M-113 armoured personnel carriers carry the mechanised infantry. The artillery have towed 105mm guns and some 155mm.

There are three countries which currently earmark forces for the reinforcement of Norway. These are: the UK, the Netherlands and the United States.

The British Royal Marines would provide some 8,000 men from 3 Commando Brigade. The Dutch contingent, also drawn from their Marine forces, are attached to this brigade and are totally integrated with the British force.

The USA would send a Marine Expeditionary Force, which could include as many as 50,000 men with 160 fighters and ground attack aircraft, 50 attack and 180 transport helicopters, 70 tanks, 100 artillery pieces and a powerful anti-tank and anti-aircraft capability.

The abilities of the UK component of this reinforcement potential are well known in Britain, having been proven in the 1982 Falklands War. The Royal Marines train specially for Arctic conditions on their yearly Norwegian deployments, as well as major exercises, and must be highly regarded by the Soviet Army.

The role of the American reinforcements is less well publicised, although it is potentially much larger. US Marine forces (and the other NATO reinforcements) would begin to move in the transition phase, with the aim of increasing readiness in the Norwegian area, maximising the available warning time, and avoid ceding any territory or vital sea areas to the enemy by default. Traditionally, this move by the USMC has been by sea, a long and possibly dangerous voyage. Certainly, a large proportion would still deploy in this manner. But in 1981, Norway and the USA signed a 'Memorandum of

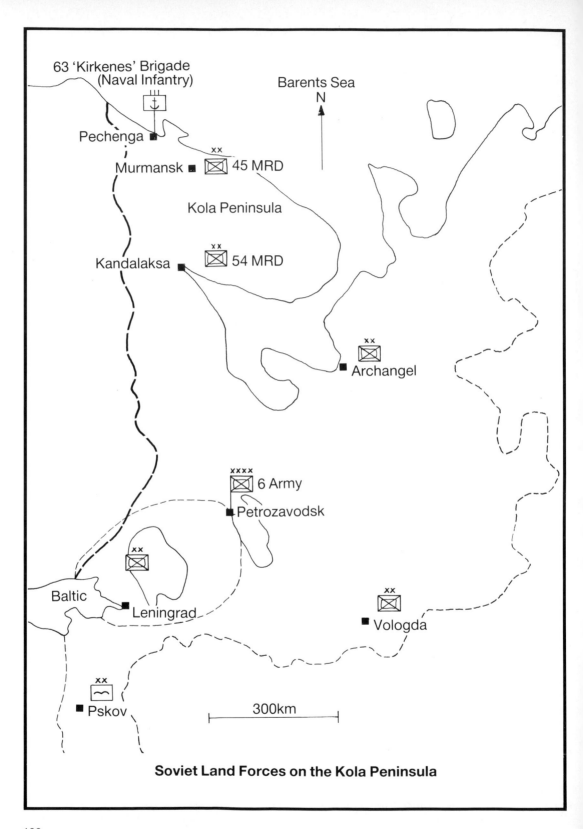

Soviet Land Forces on the Kola Peninsula

Understanding' which provided for the capability to reinforce Norway with an 'airlifted brigade-sized force' by 1989. This enhanced capability is achieved by 'prepositioning' — the placing of heavy stores, vehicles, ammunition supplies, and aviation support equipment for a complete US Marine Expeditionary Brigade on Norwegian soil. In war, the manpower for the brigade would arrive by air, collect their equipment, and deploy into the field.

This was a difficult political step for Norway to take. Although she had allowed prepositioning by British, Dutch and Canadian forces for many years, providing the same facility for the Americans was a different matter. Initially, it was proposed to stock the equipment at Tromsø, in the north. But this was too much for the Norwegian Parliament and they eventually settled on Trondheim.

This had several advantages — the central location would offer more options in a crisis: scarce transport aircraft would be less vulnerable as they arrived; and the depots would be easier to protect. But the position still means there is a 400-mile redeployment to the north. As one British officer put it, 'to establish forward dumps in Trondheim to equip troops that will fight around Tromsø is like dumping equipment in Koblenz when it will be used in Naples'.

To compensate for this, the Norwegians also agreed, as part of the same deal, to position heavy equipment for one of their own brigades in the north. In addition, the Norwegian Army will provide a considerable proportion of the logistic support for the incoming US brigade — motor transport, ambulances, engineers, etc. All in all, this move reduced the strategic airlift requirements from the US to Norway by a significant amount.

On 'Teamwork 88', the USMC units, forming 4 Marine Expeditionary Brigade (MEB), had come by sea. The organisation of 4 MEB is shown in the diagram. This US contingent included a reserve infantry battalion, roughly equivalent in status to the British Territorial Army. The differing standard of training between this unit and their regular counterparts was quite obvious. Although the Marines were certainly enthusiastic, the quality of their fieldcraft was patchy and some men appeared to be unfamiliar with the demands of the severe weather. However, it is all good experience, and, as one Marine officer said, 'they'll know what to expect next time we're here'.

The UK/Netherlands Landing Force is a specialised 'force-in-being', which can include all the following components (not all of which were deployed in 1988):

● HQ 3 Commando Brigade
● two Commandos (battalion-sized units) including one Netherlands Independent Company trained for Arctic operations
● one commando trained for mountain operations

● Netherlands 1 Amphibious Combat Group, trained for Arctic operations
● 29 Commando Regiment Royal Artillery (reinforced in war by 289 Commando Battery)
● 59 Commando Engineer Squadron (reinforced in war by 131 Commando Engineer Squadron)
● 30 Signals Regiment
● The Commando Logistic Regiment
● a light helicopter squadron operating Lynx and Gazelle
● 539 Assault Squadron including six Dutch landing craft
● the Mountain and Arctic Warfare Cadre, used as deep recce troops
● two dedicated RN Sea King helicopter squadrons, 845 and 846 Naval Air Squadrons
● when required, elements of the Special Boat Service (both Netherlands and UK).

The naval assets available in 1988 to transport and support this force included:
● the amphibious assault ships (LPD) HMS *Fearless* and *Intrepid*, each with four Landing Craft Utility (LCU) and four Landing Craft Vehicle and Personnel (LCVP)
● the six 'Sir' class Landing Ship Logistic (LSL)
● two Landing Craft Logistic (LCL)
● appropriate merchant ships ('ships taken up from trade', or STUFT). The actual shipping used in 'Teamwork' was detailed in Chapter 3.

It will be seen that only one LPD, one LSL and one LCL were missing from the exercise forces. This was an excellent effort, as was the STUFT contribution.

In order to clear the minefields the reinforced STANAVFORCHAN had moved north and was supplemented from 14 September by the 1st Norwegian Mine Countermeasures Squadron composed of the minehunter *Tana*, minesweeper *Alta* plus the two coastal minelayers *Vidar* and *Vale*. The two Norwegian combat diving team vessels *Draug* and *Sarpen* were also deployed as were half a dozen smaller Norwegian craft. The MCM forces did a good job clearing Andfiord and Ofotfiord of the exercise mine threat that had been 'laid' in the scenario by 'Orange' merchantmen and bombers.

Before the landings proper a number of other pre-assault operations were carried out, hydrographic reconnaissance, surveillance of enemy activities ashore and pre-assault landings on Rolla and Andorja. These operations involved US 'Seals' and British and Netherlands Special Boat Service and Royal Marine Mountain and Arctic Warfare Cadre personnel as well as regular reconnaissance and rifle companies of American and Royal Marines. Norwegian forces were also used. Naval Gunfire Support officers were also landed, the supporting warships having honed their skills on the Frohavet range during the Rehearsal and SACEX.

Above:
Lt-Col Slade and Maj Roddecker of VMA 542 and their AV-8B aircraft. The Harriers had landed on the Forward Operating Site (FOS) next to the E19 road just west of Bjerkvik. *G. N. Thompson*

Above right:
A LAV(AT) vehicle of 2 LAV Battalion, USMC, provides anti-tank defence as the Marines advance up the E6. The twin turret is armed with Improved TOW missiles. *G. N. Thompson*

The main American landing took place at Tovik, a small village on the Astafiord. It was unopposed by the 'enemy' forces, but heavy seas and a bitter 40kt wind meant it was no easy operation. The driving rain, heavy swell and poor visibility added to the

Below:
A Norwegian Army Leopard I main battle tank in a rather exposed position on the E6. The Norwegians provided the 'enemy' on 'Teamwork 88' and handled their tanks with great skill in the rugged terrain. *G. N. Thompson*

normal military problems of co-ordinating a major amphibious landing.

The amphibious ship USS *Nassau* steamed in the Astafiord at around 05.00 on the morning of 16 September, with several Landing Craft Utility (LCUs) trailing in her wake. Just before 06.00, 12 LVTP-7 amphibious armoured personnel carriers carrying men of 2/8th Regimental Landing Team (RLT) USMC left the assault ship and swam in the final 1,500m or so, covered by smoke and a notional air strike on the beach by two AV-8Bs.

Simultaneously, a formation of eight helicopters clattered overhead, carrying Marines of 1/25th RLT inland to their initial objective on the E6 highway, just north of Bjerkvik. Two Huey Cobra gunships escorted the troop-carrying CH-46s and CH-53s.

Once the first wave of assault troops had secured the beach at Tovik and set up defensive positions inland, the LCUs beached to disgorge their cargo of 'Hummer' jeeps, other soft-skinned vehicles and a few light armoured vehicles (LAVs). The crew of one 'Hummer' suffered the embarrassment of an impromptu ducking when their vehicle sank just after

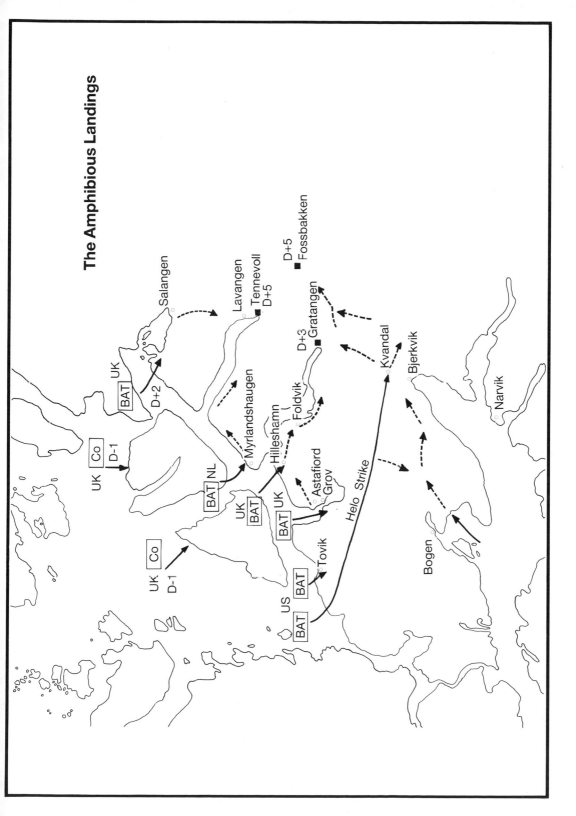

The Amphibious Landings

Salangen

Lavangen
Tennevoll
D+5

D+5
Fossbakken

UK
BAT UK
D+2

UK Co
D-1

Myrlandshaugen

Hillesshamn

Foldvik

D+3
Gratangen

Kvandal

Bjerkvik

Narvik

BAT NL

UK
BAT

BAT UK

Astafiord
Grov

Helo Strike

UK Co
D-1

Tovik

Bogen

BAT

US
BAT

111

UK/Netherlands Landing Force

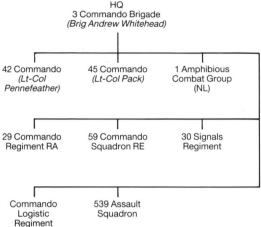

HQ
3 Commando Brigade
(Brig Andrew Whitehead)

42 Commando
(Lt-Col Pennefeather)

45 Commando
(Lt-Col Pack)

1 Amphibious
Combat Group
(NL)

29 Commando
Regiment RA

59 Commando
Squadron RE

30 Signals
Regiment

Commando
Logistic
Regiment

539 Assault
Squadron

leaving its landing craft, but overall the landing went well, considering the foul conditions.

Further up the coast at Grov, Hilleshamn and Myrlandshaugen, the assaults by 42 Commando, 45 Commando and the Dutch 1st Amphibious Combat Group (1 ACG) were equally successful. By just after 09.00, Brig Whitehead, in charge of 3 Commando Brigade, had been brought ashore by a Gazelle helicopter of the Brigade Air Squadron and was being briefed on the situation. Royal Marines of Support Company, 45 Commando were heading north along the coast road, laden down with their Milan anti-tank missiles. They were soon to need them, as 'enemy' NM-116 tanks and infantry were lying in wait a few kilometres ahead.

Other US equipment, including artillery, ammunition and other stores, were being unloaded from the 'maritime pre-positioning ship' *American Enter-*

4 Marine Expeditionary Brigade, USMC

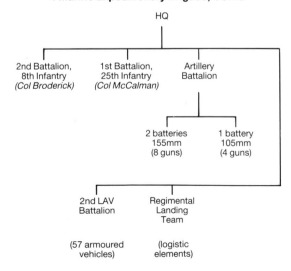

HQ

2nd Battalion,
8th Infantry
(Col Broderick)

1st Battalion,
25th Infantry
(Col McCalman)

Artillery
Battalion

2 batteries
155mm
(8 guns)

1 battery
105mm
(4 guns)

2nd LAV
Battalion

Regimental
Landing
Team

(57 armoured
vehicles)

(logistic
elements)

prise, berthed at Bogen, just across the fiord from Narvik. In particular, the rest of the 57 Light Armoured Vehicles (LAVs) of the 2nd LAV Battalion USMC were coming ashore for their first European exercise. In war, all the LAVs would have been landed tactically with the main Marine force, but exercising constraints meant this was not possible on 'Teamwork 88' and they moved on road 19 to meet the E6 at Bjerkvik.

The LAV is one of USMC's newest equipments and is already proving its worth. During 'Teamwork 88', they were everywhere, carrying out reconnaissance, providing a security screen for the Marine infantry, and giving fire support where necessary. There are three versions of the LAV — the standard LAV 25 armoured personnel carrier armed with a 25mm Chain Gun, the LAV(AT) with a turret fitted with Improved TOW anti-tank missiles, and the LAV(C) command vehicle. Their crews spoke very highly of them.

By nightfall of D-Day, all the allied forces were well established ashore. 45 Commando had reached Foldvik on the southern shore of Gratangen and had engaged the Norwegian forces there. 1/25th RLT were dug in around Kvandal, along with elements of the Regimental Landing Team and the supporting artillery battalion. 2/8th RLT was moving east through Grov, then south to Vassbotn to join the 19 road.

One platoon of the Regimental Landing Team, together with three TOW-armed 'Hummers', occupied a blocking position at Vassbotn. The Marines kept watch through night-vision goggles across a scene reminiscent of the Scottish Highlands, with a small lake by the side of the road and steep wooded hillsides rising all around. For now, all was quiet, apart from long convoys of LAVs and 5-ton trucks moving south. The weather was beginning to turn nasty again, and the Marines were glad of their British-made Goretex jackets. But high-technology was proving less reliable — the mountains were affecting radio reception.

Back at Kvandal, the calm of the night was shattered at around 04.00 on the 17th, D+1. Defying the apparently difficult terrain, several Norwegian Leopard 1 main battle tanks from Brigade North attacked the 1/25th positions near the E6, and a major battle raged for 10min or so. The aggressive handling of the Norwegian forces throughout 'Teamwork' certainly bodes well for NATO if war ever comes to the north.

The 17th dawned cold and wet. During the night the snowline had moved down about 50ft. With the US Marines about to begin their attack, the weather was, as is usual in Norway, proving as worthy an opponent as the exercise enemy. The Americans advanced up the E6 from Kvandal to Gratangen where they met the British coming down the 825 road from their landing sites at Grov and Hilleshamn.

By the 19th, Gratangen would be taken and the troops would then move up the E6 to Fossbakken by the 21st. Simultaneously the Dutch landing at Myrlandshaugen would move up the south side of Lavangen to converge with a British unit landed on the shores of Salangen on D+2 and advancing south on the 84 road to Tennevoll. Fossbakken and Tennevoll were the final objectives, putting the Blue forces in a strong blocking position across the way south by the end of the exercise.

As explained previously, land-based air support of 'Teamwork' was extensive but with a dearth of airfields in Norway suitable for fixed-wing aircraft, the AV-8B vertical take-off and landing aircraft operated by the US Marine Corps play an especially vital role.

The Marines must also have a protective aircraft carrier not too far away or must have established a workable forward airfield, otherwise they will suffer at the hands of a determined hostile air force.

On 'Teamwork 88' the US Marines practised the deployment of a Forward Operating Site (FOS) next to the E19 highway, near Bjerkvik. This was built by Marine Wing Support Squadron 274 and was used as a landing site by the USMC AV-8B Harriers of VMA542, from the assault ship USS *Nassau*. The FOS consists of two components. The first is a 72ft by 72ft square of M-2 aluminium matting, used for landing the Harriers. The other part of the FOS are fibreglass mats for taxying. The whole complex was established in about 18hr by 15 men, led by Lt Robert Deaver. This type of FOS could also, in the future, be used for the V-22 Osprey tiltrotor aircraft.

On the 'Teamwork' deployment, a refuelling point was set up at the FOS. The AV-8s took on 3,500lb of fuel in some 5-6min, sufficient for about 30min flying. After refuelling, the aircraft used the E19 as a runway. The AV-8B can take off from such an expedient strip carrying 19,000lb of ordnance. The cool climate in northern Norway contributes to a better engine performance, and no significant problems were reported with the aircraft. Twelve were being carried by USS *Nassau*, with 21 pilots.

One new and significant feature of 'Teamwork 88' was Warsaw Pact inspection. Under the terms of the 1986 Stockholm agreement on confidence-building measures in Europe, 'Teamwork 88' also saw a visit by 35 observers from 19 countries, including the USSR, East Germany, Czechoslovakia, Hungary and Poland.

All countries which are parties to the Stockholm deal are now required to give advance warning of exercises involving over 13,000 men or over 300 tanks. Equally, warning is needed for amphibious operations or parachute drops using more than 3,000 soldiers. And foreign observers must be invited to exercises of over 17,000 men. 'Teamwork 88' met the latter two criteria.

The intention is to provide a greater degree of transparency in Europe — to ensure that one country cannot make war preparations behind the mask of an exercise such as 'Teamwork'.

Below:
Norwegian Army troops on the move in M113 Armoured Personnel Carriers during 'Teamwork'.
SACLANT

7 Logistics and Convoys

Logistics cannot be neglected in either exercises or actual military operations. All the naval groups involved in 'Teamwork' carried their auxiliaries with them to keep them in action. The exercise also provided opportunities to test interoperability of equipment between allies and the use of communal NATO logistical facilities. The Dutch frigate *Crijnssen* of SNFL interchanged 76mm OTO-Melara ammunition with a 'Bremen' class frigate of the German Task Group and the *Westhinder* did the same with French type 100mm rounds with the German destroyer *Schleswig Holstein*. The Dutch auxiliary *Poolster* exchanged 40mm ammunition with the Norwegian frigate *Trondheim*. The USS *Theodore Roosevelt* provided AIM-9L Sidewinders to *Illustrious's* Sea Harriers and torpedoes to British Sea Kings which landed on the carrier. The American fleet auxiliary *Savannah* picked up (partly by helicopter) ammunition from the NATO facility at Broughton Moor in Cumbria and then moved to the NATO facility at Campbeltown to load with fuel. She was off Vestfiord a few days later and then moved to Namsos to lift more fuel from the NATO facility there. The NATO ammunition facility at Glen Douglas also provided supplies to US Navy auxiliaries, while other NATO facilities used in the exercise were Whal Bay (Iceland), Loch Ewe (UK) and Loch Striven (UK).

Ships of one nationality happily refuelled from another, including the French destroyer *Tourville* that took oil from the American replenishment oiler USS *Milwaukee*. British Royal Fleet Auxiliaries with the ASW Striking Force had no problems keeping Canadian, Dutch and American ships supplied as well as British. Special couplings allowed the British tankers to link with the Americans and Canadians. The 27,000grt German tanker *St Michaelis* was taken up from trade and fitted with an astern refuelling rig to be an ad hoc naval auxiliary. The rig was tested operationally during the exercise. Such STUFT tankers might usefully supplement NATO's overstretched reserves of naval auxiliaries in a crisis.

Even more useful than expected were the forward deployed American repair team of Task Force 137. The submarine depot ship *L. Y. Spear* at Haakonsvern carried out repairs to a British SSN and two German coastal submarines. The destroyer depot ship *Puget Sound* was much in demand given the higher than average number of bumps. The third member of the group was the salvage ship USS *Grapple*. The exercise, as we have seen, clearly demonstrated the crucial importance of this kind of afloat support to fiord operations.

Some of the logistical requirements of operations in the north can be maintained by air using Prestwick in Scotland and bases in Norway but much heavy equipment would have to come by sea. 'Teamwork 88', therefore, saw a convoy run first from Greenock to Namsos and then up the Norwegian coast to Bodø and Narvik. The convoy was made up of six ships specially chartered, the British bulk carrier *Rollness*, the British fishery protection vessel *Criscilla* (formerly the Scottish *Jura* now owned by Marrs of Hull), the German general cargo vessel *Bremer Horst Bisch* and three oil rig supply vessels, *Smit Lloyd* (Dutch), *Maersk Lifter* (Danish) and *Normand Ranger* (Norwegian).

The convoy left the Clyde on 13 September covered by MCM forces and made for Scapa Flow as a coastal convoy where it rendezvoused with four American Maritime Prepositioning Ships that had come with the Striking Fleet. These joined the convoy which sailed on the 16th before detaching south to provide a target for the concluding part of 'Teamwork', an air defence exercise in the North Sea. After Scapa the convoy became an 'ocean convoy' and had the benefit of escort from the German Task Group that came south after leaving the Striking Fleet in the amphibious rehearsal area. The German vessels, supported by maritime patrol aircraft, fought off three submarine attacks and three air strikes.

As this was an ocean convoy the commodore, a British naval officer, was in the merchantman *Criscilla* (his original intended vessel, a cable layer, had broken down). There were problems in integrating the ships, which ranged from 500 to 48,000 tons, into a single formation but the four MPS performed well and the other ships had the benefit of the experience of the passage from the Clyde. The convoy spent 9hr in single line, 12 in two columns and 43 in 'reverse arrowhead'. It made 18 turns, 14 wheels and 10 emergency turns. Zig-zagging was only ordered once by the officer in tactical command which was insufficient to practice the merchantman

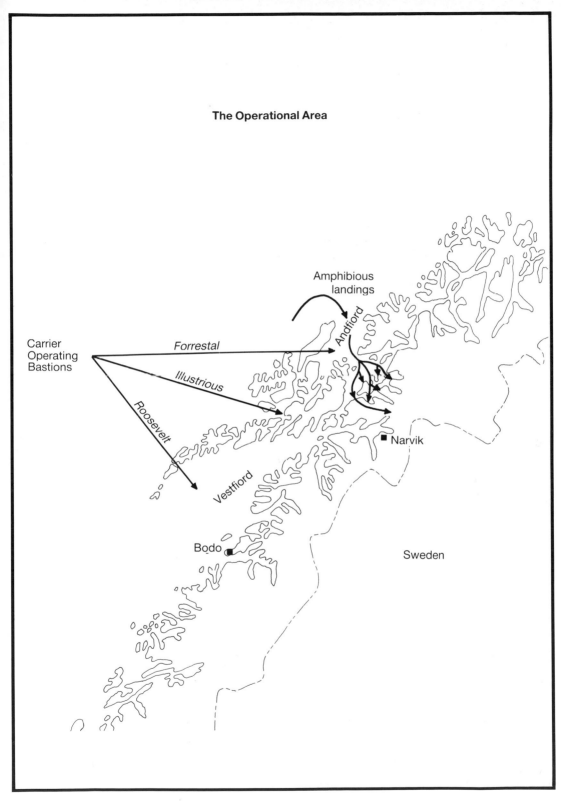

The Operational Area

Amphibious
landings

Andfjord

Carrier
Operating
Bastions

Forrestal

Illustrious

Roosevelt

Vestfjord

■ Narvik

Bodo

Sweden

Above:
The commodore's ship in the Ocean Convoy was the former Scottish fishery protection ship *Jura*, renamed *Criscilla* and owned by Marrs of Hull. She has since been leased for further fishery protection service in Mauretania. *Cdr Kristensen*

Left:
Largest ship in the convoy was the British-registered bulker *Rollnes*. *Cdr Kristensen*

Bottom left:
Smit Lloyd, a Dutch oil rig support vessel, was bound for Narvik. *Cdr Kristensen*

in this manoeuvre. One or two ships had turned the wrong way to begin with! There were two engine failures and *Maersk Lifter* fouled a fishing net; the advantage of using tug-type oil rig vessels was shown when *Normand Ranger* took her in tow while still maintaining convoy speed.

The main problems which emerged were the difficulties posed by the low levels of manning in modern merchantmen. Purely visual station keeping with binoculars, as practised in World War 2, is manpower-intensive and some ships had problems even maintaining the level of communications required. Wartime demands probably mean increasing crews by at least 20%, as planned by the Norwegians. When it came to the coastal convoy, the masters refused to do without their radar aids given the low levels of manning and the convoy could, therefore, not adopt emission controls. This is a very serious point when the decline in numbers of NATO merchant seamen is being considered. Unless sufficient manning is provided, merchant ships in convoy will announce their presence electronically to the enemy.

At Namsos, on 18 September, the ocean convoy commodore and his British staff left the *Criscilla* and a new commodore, Cdr Kristen Kristensen of the Norwegian Navy, took over. Coastal convoy commodores lead their convoys from an administrative escort vessel, and Kristensen's was the Norwegian Coastguard ship *Grimsholm*, a large converted seine-net fishing boat. The rest of the escort was provided by the Norwegian Task group, the frigates *Oslo* and *Bergen* and the Coastguard vessel *Nornen*. The frigates had been released by the concentration of the carriers and their escorts in Vestfiord. In his briefing the commodore emphasised both the narrowness of the leads up which the convoy would go and the skill of the local pilots, one of which was allocated to each ship. The aim was to arrive in Bogen Bay opposite Narvik before 06.00 on 21 September and, for exercise purposes, the safe and timely arrival of the convoy was vital to the naval activities in Vestfiord and the military activities ashore. The main threat came from submarines, with a secondary threat from mines — interference by enemy aircraft or surface action groups was unlikely.

This was the first time that a coastal convoy had been run on a major NATO exercise in Norway, an index of the greater thought being given by both NATO and the Norwegians to the logistical implications of forward operations. The commanding officer of the frigate *Oslo*, the officer in tactical command (OTC) had never protected a merchant convoy before and neither, for that matter, had Cdr Kristensen been a convoy commodore. This was to be a learning experience for everyone.

The carriers in Vestfiord were doing their job of acting as 'honeypots' for Orange submarine activity. The escorts had little information on the actual submarine threat facing the convoy but a number of areas were more likely to be dangerous than others. The tactic adopted, therefore, was for the escorts to sprint to the more probable areas and search, providing close escort when the convoy reached the area. The escorts would then sprint on again to the next danger spot. Close escort would, however, be provided up Vestfiord.

The captains rejoined their ships that afternoon after the convoy conference and the convoy weighed anchor at 19.45 and left in line, following the *Grimsholm*. There were a few problems in the opening minutes as the commodore got to grips with the problem of vessels, like the *Rollness*, that could not manoeuvre below 5.5kt and which could not suddenly stop without losing control. *Rollness* also had problems with the desired speed of 11kt and convoy speed had to be reduced to 8kt shortly after 23.00.

In the early hours of the 19th, mines were spotted ahead in Lekafiord, and the convoy made for sheltered anchorages on the other side of Austra in the inlets leading into Arsetfiord. The ships had problems anchoring but eventually suitably shallow places were found. It took until mid-morning to deal

with the mine threat but shortly after 10.30 the convoy reassembled and, led by *Grimsholm*, moved into the swept channel in Lekafiord. As they did so about midday the ro-ro *Nerrona* swept past in the opposite direction on her way south, having carried out her role as an amphibious ship. The last ship of the convoy was clear of the channel at 13.10 and 1hr later the *Bolero* came past, again on her way home after troop transport duty. *Dana Regina* later came past when the convoy was racing at 14kt across a

Below:
The Norwegian *Normand Ranger* was on home territory in the coastal convoy. *Cdr Kristensen*

Bottom:
The Danish oil rig supply vessel *Maersk Lifter* formed part of the convoy bound for Bodø.
Cdr Kristensen

Above:
Administrative escort for the coastal convoy was the coastguard ship *Grimsholm*, a converted seine net fishing vessel. *Cdr Kristensen*

Left:
The escort to the coastal convoy comprised a pair of frigates of the 'Oslo' class, including the 'name' ship *Oslo*. These ships with a heavy three-dimensional armament are well designed for coastal escort duties. *USNI*

Below left:
The other Norwegian frigate on convoy duty was the *Bergen*. Note the after armament of Penguin missiles, 3in guns and Sea Sparrow surface-to-air missiles. The enhanced importance of Norwegian coastal sea communications in NATO's overall maritime strategy adds to the rationale for Norway maintaining a significant force of coastal escorts. *Norwegian Navy*

submarine danger area, the relatively open waters off Bronnoysund. The two frigates were a comforting sight as close escort. In the middle of this area the speed once more proved too much for *Rollness* which suffered engine problems and the convoy's speed had to be reduced to 9kt. Shortly before 17.00 the convoy passed out of the danger area into more sheltered waters. Darkness had fallen by the time the convoy entered the next submarine danger area of Sandnessjoen that evening at around 21.45. Again the maximum speed, 14.5kt, was ordered and the danger was safely passed with no green flares.

Shortly after midnight the convoy reversed course due to danger ahead and another swept channel had to be negotiated. All the ships were safely through by 01.37 and Cdr Kristensen signalled to his charges that he was very pleased with them. At 03.33 the three ships bound for Bodo, *Maersk Lifter, Normand Ranger* and the big *Rollness*, detached and shortly afterwards it was decided to anchor in Mistfiord to await the best time to enter the dangerous waters of Vestfiord. The four ships moved out of this shelter in mid-afternoon in two columns, 500yd apart. The ships then moved to a waiting point until nightfall when they fell into line ahead for the dash up the fiord at 14kt.

The Striking Fleet was able to give cover with dipping sonar helicopters as the convoy, moving into three 'columns' of one ship each to diminish the target given to submarines, dashed up the southern side of Vestfiord on the evening of 20 September, the last evening of the exercise. In the event no attacks occurred and the main hazard was the minefields further up the fiord. By 03.18 the ships, now back in line, had threaded the swept channel and at 04.32, in the light of a fine early morning, the ships of the convoy were asked to move independently to their anchorages in Bogen Bay led by the

coastal minesweeper *Tista* and the German cargo ship, an apt choice as these waters near Narvik were often frequented by German warships in World War 2. Anchors were finally lowered around 05.15; the convoy had arrived on time.

It had demonstrated several things. The need for more men on board the ships to keep good lookout and attend to communications (especially in code) had been once again emphasised. More work needed to be done to find and survey safe anchorages into which ships could move smoothly. The threat had been limited as the carrier battle group had done their job diverting it away. *Oslo* had spotted a green flare in Vestfiord but it had been a long way away, in the vicinity of the carriers. *Bergen* thought she might have sniffed a submarine once. The Norwegian frigates were disappointed not to have had more 'trade' but most of the techniques of escort had been exercised, area search, close escort, safe havens, altering a convoy's speed, waiting for darkness, re-routeing, using unusual formations. It had all been most useful and enlightening.

It is not a little ironic that the Forward Strategy, which many see as an alternative to convoys, has required a new emphasis on convoy operations to sustain it. This demonstrates yet again the interdependence of battlefleet operations and the shipping movements which are both their *raison d'être* and also their lifeblood. The decline of the merchant fleets of the NATO allies and the reliable pool of trained and skilled seamen that these fleets have traditionally provided is, therefore, something that NATO's navies ignore at their peril.

8 Lessons Learned

Not everything went well on 'Teamwork 88'. The groundings and collision were most unfortunate to say the least, and unusually high for an exercise of this nature. Co-operation between naval forces and the NATO airborne early warning force proved to be more difficult than expected. The weather, especially the persistent fog, created serious problems notably to flying operations. Very quiet submarines, both nuclear and conventional, proved serious threats to surface units. The problems posed by jamming of communications to the vital synergy of platforms upon which modern naval warfare in all its complexity rests became clear. Perhaps, most important of all the vulnerability of fiord operations to the enemy mining threat if proper MCM provision is not made was emphasised.

Yet all these lessons properly learned in the months of post-exercise examination and analysis can only increase the already formidable efficiency and combat effectiveness of NATO's maritime forces. Problems, moreover, are double-edged: they affect both sides. Bad weather makes the enemy's job just as difficult, perhaps more so as he is the attacker. As well as seeing operational difficulties as a problem to be solved, therefore, their general existence should be welcomed as a vindication of the continued utility of maritime forces, including the much-maligned surface ship. Even in these days of satellite surveillance it is very difficult indeed to identify forces at sea, let alone attack them. Even if raw radar contacts can be obtained from satellites, that are themselves probably being jammed, other means must be used to identify them. This is why electronic intelligence techniques are the best means of ocean surveillance but these can be easily neutralised by the well established use of emission controls (EMCON). Therefore it is very important for merchant ships also to be able to operate in an ocean surveillance environment, which means higher than peacetime manning levels in war. All surveillance systems can also be 'spoofed' by decoys. The sea is a big place and the enemy's job of finding his supposedly vulnerable opponents can become almost impossible if he is presented with numerous likely targets from which to choose. Older surface warships can acquire a whole new dimension of operational importance when they can be made to appear, and sound, like carriers. The need to keep the seas full of potential targets will have to be balanced carefully against the needs of shipping defence in any future crisis. This is perhaps yet another reason to stress the importance of early

deployment of the Striking Fleet to its northern bastions. Covered by high levels of peacetime activity its commanders stand a much better chance of avoiding becoming tempting targets for escalation.

An important commander in any operation to insert two or three carriers into the fiords is the British Commander Anti-Submarine Warfare Striking Force. This means that the Royal Navy is still at the heart of the West's maritime strategy, despite its paucity in numbers in comparison to the US Navy. This means that the British core of ASW Striking Force must be kept up to strength, both in quality and quantity. The 'Invincible' class ASW carriers (CVSs) must operate as far as 200 miles ahead of the carrier battle groups in order to obtain quiet water for the accompanying towed arrays, and this puts a premium on their own aviation capabilities. The battle groups are formidable air forces in themselves but as big, distant organisations cannot be as responsive to requests for support as they would like to be. The colour of the pilot's suit is not the key factor in the provision of air cover. Much more important is proximity, communications, training and tasking of available assets at the time the request for support comes in. Land-based air can be as good or as bad as sea-based and is vital in all roles, surveillance, targeting and actually striking against hostile submarines, ships and aircraft. But there is no substitute for as many organic air assets as can be afforded and operated at sea.

The CVS's Sea Harriers are crucial both to defend the ASW Striking Force from enemy air surveillance and strike, as well as to act as probes to identify surface threats. They can be formidable anti-surface weapons with their Sea Eagle missiles but they cannot do everything at once. Striking still requires numbers to be effective, one reason the Royal Navy reluctantly neglected the role in the immediate postwar years. It is arguable whether SHARs are best employed in the anti-surface role, at least if air threats are likely. The advent of the anti-ship missile, especially the Tomahawk Anti-Ship Missile 'used' to good effect by US destroyers in 'Teamwork' gives both an alternative means of engaging at long-range and a supplementary capability that can be co-ordinated with air strikes, especially those mounted with insufficient forces to be certain of success. The CVS was originally going to have a small surface-to-surface missile battery but the advent of the Sea Harrier allowed it to be deleted. There is a good argument for its reinstatement, to take the pressure off the all-too-small air group. In the meantime, and ammunition stocks permitting, the Sea Dart launcher can be surprisingly useful in the surface-to-surface role also, although it is a vital AAW asset in its primary role.

The British CVSs, therefore, need powerful and modern medium-range missile batteries, both surface-to-surface and surface-to-air if they are to operate with full effectiveness. They also need the best point defences money can buy. In effect the current strategy requires the ASW Striking Force to be a latter-day 'battlecruiser force'; in 'Teamwork' Rear-Adm White was Beatty to Adm Johnson's Jellicoe. The lessons of World War 1 are clear. If one's battlecruisers are not given sufficient striking power — in the earlier case proper fire control — then, as they see the most combat at the point of the force, they are in potential danger. One would hate to see a future *Invincible* suffer the fate of her predecessor in some climactic fleet action potentially more decisive than Jutland.

The same goes for the other units in the ASW Striking Force. Operating as the vanguard of a battlefleet implies the most sophisticated air and anti-surface warfare capabilities, if not in every ship at least spread over ships within mutual support distance of each other. It is not surprising, in this context, that British frigates are expensive items of equipment. SSM capability is still important, especially at the outset of hostilities when well armed 'tattletales' and even fully fledged surface action groups pose dangerous threats unless properly countered — and one's air striking assets might have pressing business elsewhere. As stated above, missile strikes co-ordinated with other platforms are effective means of optimising available assets. The helicopters carried by the frigates — and the CVS — can also be used to call down Harpoon fire from MPA.

Adequate anti-air capability is even more important to the frigates and destroyers of ASW Striking Force. Because of other commitments ASW Striking Force did not deploy any air defence ships such as Type 42 destroyers during 'Teamwork'. The only Sea Dart launcher was in *Illustrious*. Air defence escorts would certainly be provided in war but Britain for one is getting out of the area air defence business in the longer term. Given budgetary constraints and the tendency for ASW Striking Force to operate in a dispersed formation, extending the range of point defence systems might be the most cost-effective solution, but it does seem rather a pity that the vanguard forces of the NATO Striking Fleet will not have as much opportunity to inflict attrition on the enemy air forces as the Aegis cruisers operating closer to the carriers themselves. Such air warfare vessels are battle forces as much as mere 'air defence' ships, waiting to take advantage of the emergence of the enemy fleet (his anti-ship strike

aircraft) to destroy it. One wonders if the argument over the air defence capabilities of European ships is sufficiently strategically based or the implications of the Forward Strategy sufficiently thought through. If any force is going into 'Harms Way' to do its job it is ASW Striking Force and it needs the equipment to do it. Certainly it needs its own allocated AWACS aircraft and first call on ISAR (Inverse Synthetic Aperture Radar) and other maritime patrol air assets to help it with its AAW and ASUW problems. Land-based ISAR aircraft are especially vital to ASW Striking Force in positively identifying contacts found by other forms of surveillance.

As for ASW Striking Force's main role, the anti-submarine protection of the Striking Fleet, Adm White's forces did well in 'Teamwork'. The towed array sonar systems performed magnificently with detection ranges measured in many tens of miles depending on the water conditions and the quietness of the target. During the break-in through the gaps, towed array assets were placed to optimise their detection range while the mission essential units (MEUs) were routed to minimise their chances of detection by the submarines. Such are the tactics of this subtle game of underwater hide-and-seek in which all assets must be deployed synergistically. The key to successful ASW against quiet, elusive submarines is the immediate prosecution of every sonar murmur. The main enemy, therefore, is inadequate secure communications — a problem compounded by intense jamming of the main ASW channel. More investment in secure communications would make the job of Adm White's successors a great deal easier.

Support by friendly submarines is also crucial. SSNs, as provided in the exercise, can act as powerful sonar platforms for the Striking Force, providing positive and negative information on the position of enemy boats combined with flexibility in speed and positioning without having to worry about the air or surface threats. Their firepower can also be deployed against both enemy submarines and surface ships, although longer-range missiles would greatly enhance the effectiveness of British submarines. However, the problems of immediate two-way communications with submarines remain as crucial constraints on the integration of surface and subsurface forces. Solving them would be an enormous force multiplier. Indeed if submarines ever could communicate as reliably and flexibly as surface ships with other assets, especially those in the air, *without compromising their position*, much of the need for ASW Striking Force as presently constituted would disappear. We are still a long way from that situation, however. Intervals of many hours can occur in submarine communications as the SSN dives deep. Currently, therefore, there is no alternative to a powerful CVS/towed array frigate force leading the way for the carriers. Only this force with its associated submarines can give the Striking Fleet commander the ASW advice that assures the safety of his MEUs. Possibly, of course, overriding operational priorities might dictate moving into dangerous waters relying on the close screening forces of the MEUs themselves, but the ASW Striking Force will have succeeded in its comprehensive fact-finding mission if the Striking Fleet commander fully realises the risks he is running. It is of course vital that its advice be followed.

Operating the ASW Striking Force in the busy waters close to the Norwegian coast brought its own problems of command and control, not to mention noisy water for the towed arrays. High levels of ambient noise had already proved troublesome in the Iceland basin as well as the South Norwegian sea. This noise problem also creates difficulties, as we have seen, for passive sonars actually in the fiords and it is an interesting question as to whether all these waters would have as much shipping in them in crisis or war as they do in peace. SSNs running slow and silent can hide in such conditions disturbingly easily. Conventional submarines on batteries are even harder to find but they eventually have to give themselves away when they emerge to snort. The earlier American SQR 18 towed arrays carried in US, Dutch and (with their own processing) Canadian frigates proved valuable inshore but in these noisy Continental Shelf waters active sonars — both surface and helicopter-borne — came into their own and were essential ASW assets. In Norwegian conditions however, even active sonars suffer from high reverberation, many false echoes and the strong seasonal water temperature variation. To optimise both forms of search, active-passive frigate 'combos' were exploited with some success.

For the first time HMS *Illustrious*, the ASW Strike Force command ship, joined its bigger American cousins in testing out the fiord environment, putting into Hadselfjorden to the north of the Lofotens. This is a natural and secure bastion from which to run the deep-water ASW battle off Andfiord and Vestfiord and supply helicopters to the fiord operations themselves. Both communications and flying were unaffected although the prices paid for increased protection from long-range missiles and submarines were difficulties in providing helicopter support to the towed array ships out in the open sea, and problems with air defence. Again, although things were improved in comparison with previous exercises, there were problems in consistently integrating the ASW Striking Fleet with the overall Norwegian Sea air battle. *Illustrious* was forced to rely on her own air surveillance radar and her organic AEW helicopters to fill in the overall air picture for her widely dispersed force. The AEW Sea Kings carried by *Illustrious* have some limitations in their capability but were most useful in plugging gaps in AEW cover out to sea, a further demonstration of the importance of organic assets to ASW Striking Force. This said, the support received by both maritime patrol aircraft and carrier-borne S-3s in both the surveillance and attack roles was good.

The force actually deployed in ASW Striking Force for 'Teamwork' was much smaller than that expected in actual war. The full wartime strength of ASW Striking Force is about twice that used in 'Teamwork' and every unit would be necessary for an effective defence in a real-world confrontation. Both operational British CVSs could be allocated to ASW Striking Force. This gives a number of options in the real world if not on exercise, sending one CVS group forward early to cover the UKNL amphibious force in the case of early deployment and keeping another back for precursor operations in the 'gaps'. As the latter led the main body of the Striking Fleet forward, the two CVSs could join up to provide a formidable defence to the approaches to the carrier operating bastions. The carriers can also hole up in their own fiords too, as required by the threat and the demands on their ASW helicopters.

Perhaps, *the* most impressive feature of ASW Striking Force is its international character: American, Canadian, Dutch and British units operate as one under British command. This is but one example of the quite remarkable degree of integration achieved by NATO's navies in operating together. Common communications procedures and language mean that multi-national groups can be assembled and operated virtually as easily as those of one nation. In Vestfiord the US carrier *Theodore Roosevelt* was being screened by Dutch, Canadian and Norwegian units as well as American, and this after precursor operations carried out by both of NATO's multi-national forces — as well as a Canadian group. The land-based air cover was coming from equally varied sources, including the NATO AEW force. Nothing could better illlustrate the multi-national and Alliance nature of the Forward Maritime Strategy: 'Teamwork' indeed.

The other dimension in 'Teamwork' is the amphibious component and the exercise yet again demonstrated both the viability and the importance of amphibious operations as a core element in the Forward Strategy. The retention of air bases in Norway by NATO is particularly vital, to allow the provision of air support to the integrated naval battle. Thus, the reinforcement of the Norwegian Army is crucial. Successful deployment of such reinforcement would be the deciding factor between success and defeat. As far as Norway is concerned, the availability of reinforcement is vital both to demonstrate the real commitment of the Alliance to come to Norway's defence and to secure Norwegian territory as far forward as possible. Norwegians tend to have mixed feelings about the renewed emphasis on their waters in the Forward Strategy. Since the inception of the Alliance, Norway has played a careful diplomatic role, partly due to her proximity to the USSR. Norway will not allow foreign forces (nuclear or otherwise) to be based on her soil, although this stance has been softened in recent years to allow pre-positioning of some logistic stocks. Improved shore support is being provided for forward naval operations but the Norwegians have been careful to draw the line below the level of permanent infrastructure that would offend both the Russians and Norwegian domestic opinion. Neither has anything been done to interfere with the restrictions Norway still places on Allied operations and exercises close to the Soviet border. Thus is Norway's balance of common security with its huge neighbour maintained and strengthened.

Ironically, just at the time the Forward Strategy has re-emphasised the importance of the defence of Norway and made it clear that no substantial part of that country is beyond the Alliance's defence perimeter, other developments have cast doubt over the availability of reinforcement.

In June 1987, the Canadian government published a White Paper with the results of its review of defence policy. The fate of the Canadian Air-Sea Transportable (CAST) Brigade, originally earmarked for Norway, was a central part of this review. As the White Paper explained:

'There are particularly severe problems associated with the deployment of the CAST Brigade to northern Norway. The force requires some weeks to reach Norway, making timely deployment questionable, and it cannot make an opposed landing. Moreover, once deployed, it would be extremely difficult to reinforce and resupply, particularly after the start of hostilities. The result is that, even if successfully deployed, the brigade could rapidly find itself in an untenable position.'

The Canadians decided to shift the task of the units making up the CAST Brigade from Norway to central Europe. This decision, said Canadian officials, 'was not taken lightly', and the White Paper noted that 'we did not expect unanimous support for our proposals' from the rest of NATO.

The Canadians were perfectly aware of the implications of Norway. Looking at NATO as a whole, it may not make that much difference. But for those concerned with the particular problems of defending the northern flank, it was a severe blow. In the opinion of the last British commander of Allied Forces Northern Europe, 'while we can just about get by with what we have today, we are becoming less well positioned for the future'.

NATO has been considering how best to plug the gap left by the removal of the CAST Brigade. The result will be an interesting example of an apparent setback creating the opportunity for improvement. The CAST replacement is a 'Composite Force' of Americans, West Germans and Canadians that will be at once more ready, more sustainable and more capable. Moreover, for the first time it will involve the Federal Republic directly in the defence of Norway.

There is, however, still a worrying question mark over the British amphibious capability. During the late 1970s, the British amphibious forces did not receive their 'fair share' of the defence budget. Several times, the Treasury axe hung over the Royal Marines and their specialist ships (LPDs), like HMS *Fearless* and HMS *Intrepid*. But they survived, due in no small part to their successes in the 1982 Falklands War. As things stand today, the Government is committed to retaining an amphibious capability 'in the longer term'. Various feasibility studies have examined the next generation of amphibious ships. The result, confirmed in the 1990 'options for change' review, seems to be two new LPDs and at least one aviation support ship with the possibility of other vessels, eg replacement LSLs. But a firm decision still seems as far away as ever.

In the short term, the emphasis has been on improvisation, particularly of STUFT — ships taken up from trade — such as ro-ro vessels used in 'Teamwork'. But experience on exercises has shown that such civilian ships mean less operational flexibility for the Marines — their landing craft are incompatible with the ro-ro ships' exits, and few harbours in Norway have the specialised ramps to accommodate such vessels.

This situation arises largely because of pressures on nations' defence budgets. The UK, along with other nations, is having to confront difficult choices about relative priorities. But the northern flank must be given adequate resources if NATO is to send the appropriate political signal to the Soviet Union, and if it is to continue to be able to provide the necessary military defence if deterrence fails.

As the confrontation in Europe winds down, maintaining the correct balance between deterrence and reassurance will be the main challenge facing the Western Alliance as a whole. It can learn much from Norway's record as how best to walk this particular tightrope. Some might think that the Forward Strategy runs counter to this de-escalatory trend but, in fact, this is not the case. What 'Teamwork '88' clearly demonstrated was a fundamentally defensive strategy that subtly integrates initiative and the latent threat of operational offence to constrain the offensive options of a potential attacker. Placing the carriers in the fiords transforms the defensive air picture in the north — and opens up limited offensive possibilities — just at the time that such extra deterrence is required; in normal times the perceived threat from shore-based air can remain limited and completely reassuring to the Soviets. Yet the carriers, even when they arrive, are not so threatening that they provoke the other side into premature escalation by their very presence.

In 1989-90 the USN had to accept a reduction in the number of its carrier battle groups from 15 to 14. The reduction came from the four carriers earmarked for deployment in the north.

Only having three carriers rather than four enhances stability: they create just sufficient concern without causing the other side to go 'over the top'. The air and missile threat these carriers and their escorts pose is not sufficient to disarm the Soviets in the Kola but significant enough if unopposed for the Soviets to keep the lion's share of their forces back in the North to deal with them, especially if there is a risk of nuclear escalation. It would be entirely in the Soviet naval tradition for the Northern Fleet to act as a 'fleet in being', not committing itself to a major offensive but holding itself back in case the mobile NATO naval forces tried a combat surge. The NATO forces would be themselves secure in a kind of forward Scapa Flow effectively covering both the defence of northern Norway and Atlantic shipping. As said earlier, the threat to the latter would be so reduced that a much lower scale of escort than might otherwise be required would suffice. Some escort would, however, be crucial because if there was none even a few Soviet submarines would be able to have a devastating 'Happy Time'.

If the Soviets wanted to try conclusions with the NATO battlefleet in its fiord bastions then the ball would be in their court to attack. They would in fact be very ill-advised to take on the integrated defences and allow their precious air strike assets to be minced by large numbers of naval and land-based fighters that would meet them as they tried to attack. Many of the Soviet air-launched weapons would be neutralised by the mountains. Equally, Soviet submarines would be forced to assault on more or less known threat axes, straight into the arms of ASW Striking Force. As Clausewitz pointed out the defensive is the stronger form of war; once the West's maritime forces have taken the initiative and built their fiord bastion and keeps, from which their inherent mobility means they might sally at any time, then they are too threatening to be by-passed and, perhaps, too strong to attack. The Soviet maritime threat will thus be contained as far forward as possible by a northern fortress built by maritime forces *only when and if it is required by an enemy threat*. It is hard to visualise a more inherently non-threatening overall posture.

The key to success is early forward deployment. NATO's maritime assets must be emplaced as soon as possible if they are not to suffer the fate of the attacker. The Tri-MNC contingency plan system indeed provides machinery for this. A way it might well be helped still further would be to make sure that the stabilising aspects of such forward deployment were fully understood by decision makers. NATO's navies need to go on a confidence-building offensive re-articulating their essential Forward Strategy in terms that are more in keeping with the present constructive trend in world politics. This should not be difficult, navies have traditionally played a stabilising role in world politics. Forward deployment does not mean threatened pre-emption or massive attacks on Soviet command, communication or even logistical infrastructure. This should be stated clearly and unambiguously. What forward deployment does threaten is a number of things that might concern the Soviets — limited but significant attacks on sensitive Soviet areas, a transformation of northern Norway's air defences. But these are only of significance when and if the Soviets attack. Forward deployment of NATO forces, even the potential for such deployment, also makes forward deployment of Soviet naval striking forces far too risky. The only reason NATO's deployed forces do not pose a decisive threat is the scale of the defences deployed against them. The latter therefore have to stay in place and not disappear elsewhere — eg mid-Atlantic.

It is thus crucial for NATO to demonstrate what it can do in the Norwegian Sea regularly and effectively. It plans to carry out a 'Teamwork' every other year which, with its amphibious component, will be duly notified in advance — as this year's 'Teamwork' was — under the Stockholm accords. It seems a pity that a similar notification and observation regime cannot be applied to large-scale naval exercises that do not contain amphibious forces. This would have a reassuring effect on all sides and underline the points about the stabilising character of the Forward Strategy made above. Extending the Stockholm regime to sea would help legitimise the non-threatening nature of NATO's current Maritime Strategy in the eyes of many who are still sceptical of its utility and efficacy. It would be tragic if ideas based on misunderstanding and misconception undermined the excellent work done in recent years off Norway. 1988's 'Teamwork' saw the fiord option work better than ever before and it thus vindicated both the thinking of those who re-articulated NATO's traditional Maritime Strategy over the previous decade and the commanders who have experimented with putting it into effect over the last few years. The Forward Maritime Strategy has been developed in a way that works today and that is robust enough to adjust to the new world of defensive sufficiency and common security of tomorrow. Even if, as seems likely, the US Navy moves away from emphasising forward operations against the Soviet Union, they will remain important as one option available to the west should relations with Russia deteriorate to the point that either Norway feels threatened or trans-Atlantic shipping seems hazarded. Hopefully there will never again be a need to deploy naval power in the north in the strength deployed in 1988: but the maintenance of a clear capacity to do so will continue to be needed, if for no other reason than to reassure a small ally that the welcome end of the Cold War does not mean the decidedly unwelcome abandonment of a small and loyal ally in the shadow of a large and still powerful neighbour.

Main Brace

The impressive list of forces used in Exercise 'Main Brace', NATO's first major maritime exercise in the Atlantic, held in 1952.

BLUE Forces (Under the command of Commander-in-Chief, East Atlantic)

Carrier Striking Force
United States	4 Aircraft Carriers
United Kingdom	2 Aircraft Carriers

Heavy Support Units
United Kingdom	1 Battleship
	1 Cruiser
United States	1 Battleship
	3 Cruisers
Canada	1 Cruiser

Screen
Netherlands	2 Destroyers
Norway	2 Destroyers
United Kingdom	12 Destroyers
United States	13 Destroyers
	1 Submarine

Amphibious Force
United States	1 Headquarters Ship
	4 Assault Ships
	1 Landing Ship Dock
	4 Destroyers
	1 Battalion United States Marine Corps

Carrier Support Force
Canada	1 Light Fleet Carrier
United Kingdom	1 Light Fleet Carrier
	1 Cruiser
United States	1 Light Fleet Carrier

Heavy Support Unit
New Zealand	1 Cruiser
United Kingdom	1 Cruiser
United States	8 Destroyers

Hunter Killer Force
United Kingdom	2 Fast Anti-submarine Frigates
United States	1 Escort Carrier
	5 Destroyers

Logistic Support Force
United Kingdom	1 Light Fleet Carrier
	1 Destroyer
	4 Frigates

	4 RFA Oilers
United States	7 Destroyers
	7 Transports

Convoy Escort Group
France	2 Destroyers
Netherlands	2 Destroyers
United Kingdom	2 Destroyers
	1 Frigate

Minesweeping Group
Belgium	2 Minesweepers
Netherlands	7 Motor Minesweepers
United Kingdom	8 Minesweepers
	7 Motor Minesweepers

Miscellaneous Forces
United Kingdom	2 Ships	} Convoy
United States	2 Patrol Seaplane Ships	

Under the Command of Commander-in-Chief, North

Task Force 152
Denmark	2 Frigates
Norway	4 Destroyers
	4 Frigates
	2 Submarines
United Kingdom	2 Frigates

Minesweeping Group
Norway	6 Minesweepers

Convoy
Denmark	1 Submarine Depot Ship

Under Flag Officer, Denmark

Task Force 153
Denmark	2 Destroyers
	2 Frigates
	2 Minelayers
	2 Submarines
	8 Fast Patrol Boats
	3 Motor Minesweepers

ORANGE Forces (Under the command of Flag Officer, Submarines)

Submarine Group		Baltic Group	
United Kingdom	8 Submarines	United Kingdom	1 Fast Minelayer
	1 Midget Submarine		3 Frigates
	1 Midget Submarine	Denmark	2 Destroyers
	Tender		2 Frigates
Denmark	2 Submarines		1 Submarine
Netherlands	2 Submarines	Norway	2 Destroyers
Norway	2 Submarines		1 Frigate

Raiding Group
Canada   1 Cruiser

BLUE aircraft provided by Canada, Denmark, France, Netherlands, Norway, United Kingdom, and United States

ORANGE aircraft squadrons from Royal Air Force Coastal, Bomber, and Flying Training Commands. Also from the Netherlands, Norway, and Denmark.

Below:
Last episode in the 'Battle of the Gaps' was a 'Tango' class submarine being sunk by a P-3. *Naval Forces*

Index

128